The Brazilian Dream

How I left my Finance Job in London and became an Entrepreneur in Brazil

RAPHAEL A. ROTTGEN

Copyright © 2012 Raphael A. Rottgen
All rights reserved.

ISBN: 1468135678
ISBN 13: 9781468135671

Library of Congress Control Number: 2012900045
CreateSpace, North Charleston, SC

"Twenty years from now you will be more disappointed by the things you didn't do than by the ones you did do. So throw off the bowlines. Sail away from the safe harbor. Catch the trade winds in your sails. Explore. Dream. Discover."

— **MARK TWAIN**

Contents

Preface:	Reflections On Change	VII
Chapter 1:	Born To Wander	1
Chapter 2:	Where To Go?	29
Chapter 3:	Interlude—Take Some Time Off!	91
Chapter 4:	Decision Aftermath	101
Chapter 5:	Bem-Vindo Ao Brasil	123
Chapter 6:	Settling In	137
Chapter 7:	Settling Down	163
Chapter 8:	Getting Serious	189
Chapter 9:	The Brazilian Dream Takes Off	213
Epilogue Part 1:	Concepts Of Home	223
Epilogue Part 2:	Explore, Dream, Discover, And Write About It	225

Preface: Reflections On Change

Why am I not on the beach right now? I cannot seem to think about anything else anymore. The mental image becomes clearer and clearer: I'm lounging in one of those typical deck chairs that you can rent anywhere on the beach in Rio de Janeiro for about two dollars, staring lazily at the hills in the background, sipping a passion fruit *caipirinha* that you can buy for about three dollars from the same guys who rent you the deck chairs. My feet are semiburied in warm white sand. A gentle breeze from the Atlantic Ocean makes the ninety-plus temperature ever so pleasantly bearable. In the background the waves are crashing in a constant rhythm, their noise only regularly interrupted by the calls of the various salespeople, peddling anything from sandwiches to Brazilian-style scant bikinis and hippie jewelry. My favorite is the guy selling pineapple whose sales technique is to sneak up on sunbathers from behind and startle them by screaming "abacaxi!" (the Portuguese word for "pineapple"). Then I hear the Skype jingle.

The Skype jingle?! Yes, the Skype jingle. I crash out of my daydream and find myself sitting at my desk and staring at a massive spreadsheet that I have already spent the past few hours refining. My desk is cluttered with a patchwork of papers that I should sign or review or probably just throw away. It is a Friday, just after four in the afternoon —according to research, the productivity low point of an average day— and indeed my productivity has fallen off a cliff. All I can think about is that weekend trip. I need a coffee, a big coffee, to reenergize myself for the rest of the workday. This all seems so familiar, *too* familiar…am I having déjà vu?

Then it strikes me: I *am* having déjà vu. I have lived this type of moment before, so many times. Just a few years earlier, in 2007, if I had not been traveling at the time, I probably would have been sitting in my office on London's Curzon Street. Because I was working in an equity hedge fund at the time, I almost certainly would have been reviewing a financial analysis in a spreadsheet, and right about now there would have been the same thought about a big coffee: a grande soy latte at the Starbucks on Berkeley Square. I probably would have been daydreaming about a weekend trip too, maybe to Barcelona or Croatia, especially if it was during one of London's bleak and gray winters.

Those nostalgic thoughts stop, though, as I become acutely aware of my surroundings again. The sun is blazing in from the outside, where it must be in excess of ninety degrees. This is certainly not London autumn weather. I am in São Paulo, Brazil's largest city and economic center. I am not sitting in a cubicle, but in an eclectically decorated private office. My desk is an enormous kidney-shaped steel piece of furniture that I salvaged from a commercial property that I recently bought for investment. Besides my laptop and the patchwork of papers, there is a bowl of frozen açaí berries (an überhealthy fruit from the Amazon). There are various frames on the walls, one of which includes a photo of me and Brazil's former President Lula at a recent wedding of friends of ours; several others include clippings of magazine reviews of JA367, a São Paulo lounge bar, of which I am part owner. Even my laptop screen is, at second glance, quite different from what it would have looked like in my London days. The financial model I am working on is not for some random company, but it is for my own company, in whose headquarters I am sitting. It is also entirely in Portuguese. The other two windows open on my laptop are my e-mail and a travel website. That probably would have been the same in London. However, while in London most of the e-mails would have been from my boss asking me to do something, now most of them are from people responding

PREFACE: REFLECTIONS ON CHANGE

to my requests for them to do something as, for better or worse, I am the boss now. I probably receive many more e-mails now than I used to, but they are often about more interesting things than the messages about company earnings revisions or new analyst opinions that I used to receive in London (albeit I now also receive e-mails about broken air-conditioning, staff faking sick days, and a range of other things that I could really do without). The e-mails, too, are all in Portuguese. I am using a travel website to plan my weekend trip, as I probably would have done in London too. However, instead of flights to Barcelona, I am checking the timetable and prices of the air shuttle between São Paulo and Rio de Janeiro. In the world of air shuttles, I tend to believe this is the most attractive one around. Forget New York to Washington. The flight time between São Paulo and Rio is about thirty-five minutes. Because both cities have domestic inner-city airports, the door-to-door travel time can be as little as two and a half hours. Imagine leaving your office in New York and dropping into a deck chair on South Beach in Miami just two and a half hours later.

I still need that big coffee, so I walk out of my office, which is located on the second floor of a 1940s former residence of some four thousand square feet in Pinheiros, a centrally located neighborhood in São Paulo. My secretary hands me a bunch of mail, mostly bills, just as a reminder that *that* part of my life has not changed. I did not need to be reminded that my life was still full of responsibilities. The employees crammed into the house's various rooms—for whose livelihoods I feel responsible—are a powerful enough reminder of the fact that my move to Brazil was never about escapism and leaving everything behind. I have more responsibilities now than ever before in my life, by choice.

I keep on thinking about all of the things that have changed, and those that have not, during the twenty-minute walk to the nearest Starbucks (fortunately it has recently entered the Brazilian market, providing me and the expat community with a cozy feeling of cultural and temporal continuity; however, its network density still leaves a lot to be desired—hence the twenty-minute walk).

Why and how did I come to Brazil?
How did I get to run a start-up company?
How the hell did I end up owning half of a cocktail bar?
And how come I am thinking all of this in Portuguese?!

It is not only I asking these types of questions nowadays. Friends and acquaintances from London, New York, and other places outside of Brazil are asking them too—in ever-increasing numbers—especially since economic events in recent history have shaken up the foundations of many an established life abroad. It is partly with those friends and acquaintances in mind that I decided to write this book, which is intended to be a mixture of storytelling and practical advice for those contemplating a similar move.

In my opinion, I am writing this book inappropriately early; I feel the most exciting chapters of my time in Brazil are yet to be written, and I still have many dreams I would like to realize here. However, I believe that Brazil is one of the most exciting places in the world *right now* and, sensing a spirit of adventure in at least some people to explore the option of building a new life here, I would be very happy if my story could end up helping their thought process just a bit.

The book is organized largely chronologically, but especially in the beginning, the chronological division also tends to mirror a thematic division. Chapter 1 tries to summarize how in my mind certain aspects of my life and character have primed me to take the major step of emigrating to a different country. Some may well find this chapter slightly too personal. I am sincerely the last person who thinks that his personal life is so interesting that it should be forced on the wider world in written form; I happily leave that to the Justin Biebers of the world. However, emigrating is a significant life decision and, probably more than any pragmatic

PREFACE: REFLECTIONS ON CHANGE

consideration, those contemplating doing it should think about whether their character and personality is compatible with the process. There probably exists a psychological questionnaire that could test this in a scientific way, but since I did not bother to find it, I figured I would just reveal some of my own character and personality traits and let the reader reflect on whether he or she could be a candidate for the type of move I have made. Chapter 2 explains how I chose where to go. It is the chapter that is most like a guidebook in that it lays out the methodological road map that I had devised for arriving at my decision. If you have the luxury of choosing where to go, you should read this chapter with particular attention. In Chapter 3 I argue that you should try to take some time off before your move and do something (or several things) that you have always wanted to do. Chapter 4 explains my experience of leading with some of the things that will immediately follow your decision to move—whether they are merely practical, such as moving logistics, or emotional, such has handling doubts about the decision. The remaining chapters relate my experience of arriving and building a life in Brazil. They do so in chronological order but touch on every major realm of life, including work, friends, romance, hobbies, and language. The book closes with a couple of brief chapters, one that contains my reflections on what "home" is, and another with some final thoughts about emigration in general.

I hope that for whatever reason you picked up this book, you will get something out of it. If you have any questions, thoughts or comments, feel free to post them on the book's Facebook page at www.facebook.com/thebraziliandream.

Happy reading! Or, as we say here, *boa leitura!*

SÃO PAULO, DECEMBER 2011

CHAPTER 1

BORN TO WANDER

So how did I decide to leave a very compelling job (investment analyst in a hedge fund) in a very compelling city (London) to move to a city relatively unknown to me (São Paulo), without having any job? And I should add that I moved in late 2007, leaving my job in March 2007, by many standards perhaps the peak of the bull market, a time when, politely speaking, it seemed incomprehensible to leave everything behind that I decided to leave behind. Less politely, it seemed nuts, somewhere on the same craziness level as leaving finance and joining a monastery.

I did not come to Brazil in the way that many other foreigners used to arrive here—on a temporary company posting (i.e., as the traditional expat). There is nothing wrong with coming here on a company posting; if it had happened to me, I would have happily accepted it. Many of my local friends did come on company postings. However, my story is different. I made an independent, unforced, conscious, some say rebellious decision to move from London to São Paulo. I am a twenty-first-century emigrant.

I should also point out that there was no plan. At least in the beginning. In the end, there was a very detailed "execution plan" of the move, about which I shall talk further on.

I believe my emigrating to Brazil and building a new life in São Paulo is a confluence of my personal history, some catalytic factors, and, as usual, a good measure of serendipity and luck.

I have been lucky and privileged in that my life had primed me for being a potential emigrant at some point. From an early age on, my family had insisted on taking me on as many trips abroad as possible, believing travel to be one of the best forms of education that life has to offer. My first long-distance journey, at eight years of age, was when my family went to New York, Miami, and—an eight-year-old's dream—Disney World, at the time flying with now-defunct Pan Am. By the time I graduated from high school, I was lucky enough to have been to four continents and to speak three languages. Although, all this time I had continued to live in the same country, Germany, Wanderlust had been irrevocably instilled in me.

When it came to choosing a university, I wanted to leave Germany and immerse myself in a new, different environment, despite all of the challenges this might bring, or, more likely, *because* of all the challenges. I chose to enroll at the Wharton School of the University of Pennsylvania in Philadelphia to study business administration. I had loved the United States ever since my parents had sent me to spend the summer in Florida with American family friends at the age of thirteen. Albeit it was only for four weeks, and the elderly couple of family friends did their best to act as substitute parents in every way, it still imbued a sense of independence in me, and I vastly improved my English (the original idea of my parents), even though it left me with a temporary southern accent. On the downside, I came to know, and became temporarily somewhat addicted to,

McDonald's as well as various other American fast-food chains and ruined my nutrition for a while. It was the first time in my life that I had come to a new country, a new culture, without friends, and without a fluent command of the local language. It was also the first time that I embraced a new culture, made new friends, and gained fluency of a local language. It would definitely not be the last time.

And so in summer 1993, I embarked on my first international move, leaving Germany for university in Philadelphia, with three suitcases, my smallest move ever. I was the first person in my family to go to university abroad, and one of two in my high school graduating class of fifty-four.

PHILADELPHIA, 1993-1997

I arrived at the University of Pennsylvania (known simply as "Penn") speaking fairly fluent English; in fact, I had been at the top of my English class in my German high school. Nevertheless, it was a change in gear. My life went from speaking, on a daily average basis, approximately 90 percent German and 10 percent English (and some French thrown in there) to speaking virtually 100 percent English. In my high school intensive English class, I had been writing papers of approximately fifteen pages in length and had actually felt quite good about them. Now I found myself in a mandatory English literature class, being the only non-native speaker, and the expected length of papers was in excess of thirty pages; I literally ran out of vocabulary. There were other minor "adaptation hiccups," such as my repeated failure, again, to take into account how easy it is to end up with a bad diet in the United States. I would start with breakfast at McDonald's and would eat a tub of Ben & Jerry's ice cream every night while studying—and I gained some twenty pounds by the end of that year. At my first house party, I got to know, unwittingly, the American college tradition of Jell-O shots (small portions of jelly that are made with vodka instead of water, meaning that every one was the equivalent of a vodka shot, with the fruit flavor masking the alcohol pretty efficiently). Feeling hungry after two hours of dancing at the party, I was happy to see the "dessert table" and had about ten Jell-O shots in ten minutes. The next thing I remember was waking up in the morning on the floor of the empty house.

Yet I adapted and I enjoyed it. As would become a recurring pattern in similar future situations, I formed a core group of local friends who helped me in this process, whether it was by proofreading my papers in the beginning or the arguably more important task of teaching me American dating etiquette. However, one of the benefits of Penn was that there were not only Americans. In fact, Penn was—and to my knowledge, still is—the most international of the Ivy League colleges, with some 10 percent of the student body coming from outside the United States. At Wharton (the university's business school), this percentage was even higher. Among my friends were any number of Europeans, Brazilians, a disproportionate number of Turks, Russians, Indians, Chinese, and the first ever student from Estonia.

After three and a half years, I left Penn with two degrees (finance and psychology), a raft of new friends, countless new good and bad memories, about the same weight that I had when I arrived (fortunately I had managed to adjust my nutrition, and I also took up sports again), a solid American-accented English with the capability of writing papers of many more than thirty pages, and a job with Wall Street blue-chip bank J.P. Morgan. I also left feeling half-American and having lost any sort of fear of adapting to new cultures or making big moves.

My job with J.P. Morgan was in New York City. Being one of a rare breed—a German with a Penn/Wharton degree—and with investment banking booming in post-unification Germany at the time, there was no shortage of opportunities to go work in Germany, but I never seriously considered this. New York was the undisputed capital of the world, the nerve center of global finance, a city that I had loved when I first visited it at eight years of age with my parents, and now I held an entry ticket to go and live there. I sensed my own personal American Dream. By the way, while, at the time, I thought I was adventurous for choosing a New York finance job over, say, a Frankfurt finance job, it really, objectively speaking, was not an adventurous, but rather a conventional choice. It was what one did as a Wharton graduate. The truly adventurous options would have been to head to an Internet start-up (this was 1997) or to a hedge fund, then a fledgling, nimble industry. However, I did not have the chutzpah or the vision at the time to do this. It is something that I remember—not so much with regret, but simply as something to reflect on—especially with regard to similar choices in the future between conventional and unconventional options.

NEW YORK CITY, 1997-1998

I arrived in New York City driving a U-Haul moving van with my few university student possessions, mostly books and clothes and no furniture. I chose location over space with regard to my new rental apartment and predictably ended up in a "shoe box"-sized studio of some two hundred and fifty square feet on the city's Upper West Side, close to Central Park. New York, like London, is a fascinating place to live at any moment in life, but I think it is particularly so at a still formative time like your twenties. It is full of people from all over the world who have come in search of some dream and bring their own cultures and backgrounds along, enriching the city and its inhabitants. Whatever life experience you are in search of, you will probably find it somewhere in New York. I always thought that if I ended up not having the money to take my kids on extensive international trips, I would at least try to raise them in a place like New York—a place that is like one-stop shopping for the diversity and richness of the world.

Adapting to life in New York was not difficult: I had simply moved from one big American city to another, and the basic elements of life remained as much the same as the chain stores that I frequented for shopping. After a short stint in J.P. Morgan's debt capital markets department, I joined the mandatory one-month new analyst training program. All new analysts from J.P. Morgan offices around the world—including New York, London, Frankfurt, Hong Kong, Paris, and Tokyo—were required to take part in this program in New York. Between the seventy of us, we must have spoken some twenty languages and came from about a dozen different ethnic groups. While there were some native New Yorkers in the program, for most of us it was the first time that we would *live* in New York City. We worked very hard during the day but at night tried out restaurants, bars, clubs, karaoke places, concerts, theaters, and the occasional strip club. It was the magical initial phase of getting to know a new city, something that I can compare only to the initial highly passionate phase of falling in love, before a relationship moves into a more "settled" phase. It is something that I experience with every new city after moving. There is an important general point here: It is pretty easy and normal to find a new city exciting for about up to six months. Then, after you have been to all the cool restaurants, clubs, theaters, and museums, you better find a reason why you will continue to like the city as a home.

My love affair with New York eventually moved into the "settled" relationship phase. I got a roommate and moved into a bigger apartment, still on the Upper West Side; I joined a gym next to the office; I found a doctor, dentist, and hairdresser; and—most important— the training program ended, and I entered the brutal work routine of an investment banking analyst. Because I was a first-year analyst in mergers and acquisitions, widely regarded to be the toughest of work environments in the investment banking world, this meant on average ninety- to one-hundred-hour workweeks. For the most part, I tried to take Saturdays off, but weekdays meant work from 09:30 a.m. to 02:00 a.m. and Sundays from around midday to midnight. Somehow my coworkers and I managed to keep going and tried our best to have a balanced life; I would skip out to go to the gym around 10:00 p.m. after my boss went home, come back around midnight to finish up work, and then meet friends for a drink around 03:00 a.m. The energy of the city seemed to keep us going. I even managed to have a girlfriend, predictably from J.P. Morgan as well, as it was pretty much impossible to have time to date anybody from outside the firm. Life, in all aspects, was very intense. In some ways, this was good, but in other ways, the intensity of the work routine also meant that the lifestyle would "get old" rather quickly. I got some occasional relief when I picked up a project that required me to spend many weeks on a deal in Canada. The temporary change in environment was very welcome, even though I did not actually get to know the city because I went from airport to office to hotel to office to airport. Nevertheless, both my girlfriend and I had a growing feeling that a change of scenery was needed— new jobs, in a new city. So we started to think about and plan that move.

Our first trip together as a couple was to London and Paris, and one of our favorite activities was hanging out in the crêperies in Saint-Germain. Being typical, indoctrinated investment bankers, we assigned code names to any type of projects, including to our new project of moving (M&A bankers give code names to everything, for confidentiality reasons), and we ended up calling it Project Galette, the name for the savory version of crêpe (besides, *crêpe* sounds too much like *crap* in English). We bought a whiteboard for the apartment we shared in New York and started to brainstorm and later strategize all elements of a potential move, principally which cities were options, and what jobs we could realistically have in those cities. It was the type of brainstorm-from-scratch that I would later repeat before moving to Brazil. The other similarity between Project Galette and my move to Brazil was that these were the only two of my international moves that were decided with a partner. Both of those times I was happy to have another person brainstorming and planning together with me, adding things on that whiteboard, and occasionally crossing something out assertively. On our whiteboard, we soon matched up initial wild wishes ("Let's move to Paris!") with reality ("Where can we find good jobs?") and identified a clear target city that remained ("London," circled in red, and "Paris," crossed out).

Because we were both still at a stage in life without meaningful accumulated financial resources, and also because my American girlfriend needed a working visa to live in London, our key task was to find jobs before moving, so this is what we focused our energies on. The even more meaningful limitation than money was time, as we were both working those ninety- to one-hundred-hour weeks, and *holiday* was a dirty word in investment banking. Hence we decided that we would need one week of intense interviewing with as many firms as possible in London, and we would take that week off by essentially faking family emergencies at work. And so it went: we chose who we thought was the best headhunter, did as many preliminary phone interviews as possible—clandestinely hiding away in little-used conference rooms—scheduled a week packed with interviews in London, and, when the time came, literally ran out our offices because of some unspecified family emergency. Nothing ever goes smoothly, of course. On the way from the office to the airport, first a drug addict drew a knife on my cab driver and then I fell asleep on the subway, waking up in the Bronx. Somehow we still made it to London.

Things went according to plan, and we both soon accepted job offers, my girlfriend with Credit Suisse, and I with the brand-new London office of American boutique bank Greenhill, where I was one of the first employees in the new London office. Greenhill was a unique opportunity, effectively to work in a start-up environment in investment banking (the London office at the time had fewer than ten employees).

LONDON, 1998-2000

We arrived in London in October 1998, having had less than a week off between jobs, which, retrospectively, is way too little. As I will elaborate, moves should be seen as an opportunity to take some time off from your usual routine. The move was as easy as it possibly could have been. In the end, we stayed in basically the same jobs (just with different companies), we still lived in an English-speaking environment, and London offered basically all the same big-city advantages as New York City, in terms of culture, nightlife, restaurants, and infrastructure. I think one of the hardest adjustments was dealing with what we perceived to be a drop in general customer service quality between the United States and the UK. And then there was the weather. Both of us loved the English summer, including all the English summer events such as Wimbledon tennis, Henley rowing, and Ascot horse racing, but from about October to March each year, we virtually developed seasonal affective disorder because of the short and dark days. I felt like trying one of those therapies where they shine colored lights in your face. Our preferred relief from this problem was to take weekend skiing trips. One of the great advantages of living in London is the number of weekend trip options within a radius of one- to three-hour flights—you can pretty much go anywhere in Europe, and even North Africa. We also explored London's theaters, concerts, restaurants, bars, and clubs. During the daytime, however, we were back in our investment banking working routines, albeit with slightly better hours than those in New York City. By the following summer, we both got promoted to the next level in our firms.

With work going well, and all of London's nonwork diversions, the thought of moving again never sprang to mind, at least during the first two years there. However, as life goes, I did not have to proactively make that choice; it came about by circumstance. Specifically, one of Greenhill's main clients retained the firm to sell off a major subsidiary in Australia. In the summer of 2000, a team from Greenhill, including me, headed down for local kickoff meetings in Sydney, very conveniently timed to coincide with the first week of the Sydney Summer Olympic Games. While we had some meetings, work in Sydney in general predictably had ground to a halt, and I soon found myself watching track and field in the Olympic Stadium. After slightly more than a week, we headed back to London, and at that time my expectation still was that the Australia project would involve occasional trips to Sydney, but not more. However, my bosses asked me to take care of the project's day-to-day operations in Sydney, probably in part because they wanted to provide good local coverage to our client, but also did not want to take the twenty-four-hour flights from London to Sydney too frequently. In a serendipitous circumstance, my relationship was coming to an end around this time, so the decision to move to Sydney for the duration of the project was not exactly difficult.

SYDNEY, 2000-2001

In August 2000, I "moved" from London to Sydney, albeit, of course, it was not a traditional type of move. I brought only a minimum of things and left most of my stuff in London. In Sydney, I started out staying in a hotel in the city center for the first month and lived out of two suitcases. I stayed in Sydney for only eight months, until March 2001. However, I still consider myself as having "moved" to Sydney at the time, in an expat sort of way, because a large part of my life did move to Sydney. By virtue of the people I met on the deal, and via introductions of various friends from London and the United States, I was lucky enough to have had a rudimentary social network from the very beginning. Soon I regularly went to parties, whether at somebody's apartment in town, or at beach houses, or on sailboats on and around Sydney Harbour.

After having stayed almost one month at the traditional and very comfortable Observatory Hotel in the Rocks, an old neighborhood near Sydney's central business district,

I seized the opportunity to move into the apartment of a friend, who had gone traveling for several weeks, on Tamarama Beach, one of Sydney's most glamorous small beaches, and just one beach over from famous Bondi Beach. It was the first time in my life that I lived in a beach city, and I loved every part of it. I adapted to the beach lifestyle like I was born for it. Warm-weather beach cities around the world, such as Sydney, Cape Town, Rio de Janeiro, and LA, have a strong focus on physical activity and body culture. At the time I was a sedentary, desk-dwelling investment banker, weighing in at just over two hundred pounds. In Sydney, after taking just a few walks on the beaches and seeing scores of Sydney men with six-packs playing beach volleyball, surfing, or running, I felt like I had to do something if I wanted to have a shot at ever dating again. So I took up running regularly. By November 2000, I had signed up for the London Marathon in April 2001, and virtually every morning before work I would get up and run. While I was still staying at the city center hotel, one of my favorite runs was a roughly ten-kilometer course that ended on Bondi Beach, where I would take a quick swim before taking the bus and train back to the city and going to the office. By the time I moved to the beach, I had worked my way up to thirty-kilometer runs (my preferred course for that distance was a run from Bondi to Manly, Sydney's other famous beach, crossing the iconic Sydney Harbour Bridge roughly halfway).

By December I had also moved on from my life in London in terms of physical appearance—I had lost more than twenty pounds of weight, and I was rather suntanned. There was no seasonal affective disorder, as I had moved from Northern to Southern Hemisphere at the right time; I completely skipped winter that year, enjoying first the London summer and, soon after, the Sydney summer. In another adaptation to the local lifestyle, I took up surfing. First it was just a few lessons, but soon I bought my own board. I never managed to get up more than perhaps ten seconds, but I did not care either; it was the best feeling in the world. I would sleep with the curtains and windows open, hearing the waves crash at night, wake up with the first rays of the morning sun hitting my face in bed, grab my board, and head out to catch a few waves in the morning, before going to the office. My work colleagues in London did not want to hear one more thing about it. The evenings remained fun too. Sydney has an amazing gastronomic scene. I bought the local restaurant guide and made a point of visiting as many restaurants as possible. I started dating locally, first rather casually, but by Christmas 2000, I spent the holidays with an Australian girlfriend and her family in Byron Bay, a bucolic beach resort in northern New South Wales, about thirty minutes by air north of Sydney. I spent New Year's 2000/2001 on a boat in the middle of Sydney Harbour. In February I participated in the street parade of the famous Sydney Gay & Lesbian Mardi Gras, which was a rather unique experience.

Of course, all investment banking deals come to an end, as did ours, in mid-March 2001, and so I had to return to London. My Australian girlfriend and I made a short-lived halfhearted attempt at maintaining an ultralong-distance relationship, which was predictably doomed by the twenty-four-hour flight time distance. I actually did not go straight back to London, as my boss had conceded me some days off after the intense final phase of the deal. I spent a few days in Queenstown in New Zealand, which I already knew, where I cycled and bungee-jumped, among other activities. Then I decided to stop over in a place where I had never been and hardly knew anything about—Tokyo. I only spent one night in Tokyo, but I remember how different everything was and how far fewer people spoke English than I had thought, based on my experience in other Asian capital cities. It actually made me feel uneasy, and I did not anticipate returning to Japan. Little did I know that only one and a half years later I would move to Tokyo.

BACK TO LONDON, 2001-2002
First, however, I returned to London, and the reintegration into London life was very easy. I moved into a triplex flat in Covent Garden together with a colleague and friend from Greenhill. I was about to have my third consecutive summer season (because of the switch in hemispheres), and I was single. Australia had left its marks on me—I never again stopped running, and I completed the London Marathon in April 2001. Workwise, I fell back into the M&A routine at Greenhill, and frankly very soon I felt bored. This was not lost on my very perceptive bosses, and in November 2001, one of the two senior London partners called me to his office and offered me the chance to move to Greenhill's New York office and to work in the brand-new restructuring group. Having caught wind of this, only one day later, the senior partner of Greenhill's Frankfurt office offered me the opportunity to work in Frankfurt. So there I was again with virtually the same choice that I faced when I graduated from university—New York or Frankfurt. There were some good arguments for Frankfurt again: the German M&A market looked very good, I had done my stints in New York and London, and Frankfurt was a small office where, given my background and experience, I probably could have a rapid impact and progress quickly. Besides the purely professional angle, Frankfurt was also the place where I had not lived yet; New York I already knew. But I was not "done" with New York. I felt a strong urge, a gut feeling, that I should live there again, and not in Frankfurt. I could not really explain why, but I also did not owe anybody an explanation, so I went with my gut feeling.

NEW YORK CITY, 2002
So it was back to New York City in February 2002, about three and a half years after I had left. This time I opted to live in Chelsea in order to get to know at least another neighborhood, even if it was the same city. Because it was three and a half years later in my career and because I

was sharing my apartment, it was no longer the size of a shoe box, but a two-bedroom on a high floor, with a clear view of the Empire State Building. I slotted back into New York life almost overnight; I still had many friends in the city, and many of my favorite restaurants and bars were still around. There were some minor changes besides my living in a new neighborhood. My office was on Park Avenue rather than on Wall Street, I joined a new and different gym, I started spending much more time than before in Central Park as I continued to run regularly, and I spent my first summer in a shared house in the Hamptons, the Long Island beach escape of Manhattanites. In my social life, besides just meeting up again with old friends, I followed my old technique of getting introductions for new friends from friends in other places, mostly London. One of those introductions led to a new girlfriend. At work, my bosses' plan to reignite my motivation by assigning me a new challenge worked, as I enjoyed learning about and working in the restructuring of distressed companies. I also quite simply enjoyed the fact of being surrounded by new people at work. In late spring 2002, our restructuring team successfully pitched to be the advisors of the bondholders of a distressed UK telecom company. As the vast majority of work on this deal was done in London, I found myself, quite ironically, spending workweek after workweek in London, while only coming back to New York on the weekends, where often I would head straight to the Hamptons. I seemed to use planes like commuter buses, and the Sanderson hotel in London was like a second home for me. I must say that, much to the chagrin of my New York girlfriend, I enjoyed commuting between London and New York, as it allowed me to keep in touch with my friends in both places and take advantage of both cities. I guess it is the kind of situation you love when you just cannot make up your mind in which city you want to live. Of course I knew this could not last forever, as it would only go on as long as the deal went on, and privately I could surely not afford this type of weekly travel.

In general, though, I was happy with my life in New York/London, and I did not really foresee or proactively plan any major change. I felt that I was getting "settled," my career was on a good track, and social life was good.

Just then, though, life intervened in the form of a headhunter. The partner of a London headhunting firm, via a referral of a friend of mine, cold-called me with the opportunity to join a brand-new hedge fund. Headhunter calls were nothing uncommon, probably a monthly, and sometimes even weekly, occurrence, but typically they involved the offer to move within investment banking to one of the bigger firms, such as Merrill, Goldman, or J.P. Morgan. This was not something that was compelling to me, having gotten used to the small firm, yet high quality, environment of Greenhill, and I never had any hesitation to say "no," even to the request for a preliminary conversation. The hedge fund opportunity was different though. While at the time of graduation from Penn I did not have the vision or guts to join a hedge fund, my circumstances had changed over the past five years: I had savings allowing me to take a risk, and I had learned a lot more about the industry, mostly because some friends had made the move from banks to hedge funds. Most important, and somewhat serendipitous, the key client on my deal at Greenhill at the time was a hedge fund, allowing me to look at its work at least from the outside in. And its work seemed more interesting than my work, apart from the fact that it appeared so inherently more compelling being the client of an investment banker rather than the investment banker. I had also become aware of the earnings potential that hedge funds held if (and this was clearly a big *if*) one performed well. All in all, the proverbial grass on the other side not only looked somewhat greener, but it looked like a golf course green. This impression only grew stronger as I went through the interviewing process and realized just how multinational the team was.

The portfolio manager of the fund was an Italian American who had already lived in various countries and spoke five languages; the other members of the initial team included a Canadian, an Australian who had lived in Japan for a while and spoke fluent Japanese, a Brit, a Hong Kong Chinese, a Frenchman, an Italian, a Japanese, and a Korean. It was multinational and diverse by design and right up my alley. There was one key twist in the job proposal: while my eventual job was going to be a European equities analyst in the future London office of the new fund, everybody would spend an initial period in Tokyo, as this was where the fund manager was based and, more important, in order to mold the team together in this critical initial phase. Besides, Asia was half of the fund's investment focus, albeit not mine. My only experience with Tokyo was my short visit about one and a half years earlier, and I remembered my feeling from the time—that it was not a place where I naturally felt at ease, because of the difference in culture, because of the lack of English speakers, and so on. My affinity with Japan at the time was the weekly visit to a New York or London sushi bar. However, this uneasiness was the only remaining small obstacle in making my final decision—and I was biased toward wanting to overcome this obstacle, as I was by now convinced the new job opportunity was the right risk at the right time. If it had only been about a job change, or even a job change with a "lesser" move (let's say New York back to London, or New York to San Francisco), I would have had already signed the offer. Of course, the way to change your mind (or strengthen your existing impression) about a place is to simply go there again, and this is what I did, as part of a long weekend in Tokyo, after the fund manager had already made an offer to me and was basically trying to convince me to accept it. One Friday in London, instead of taking the evening flight back to New York as usual, I hopped on a flight to Tokyo, traversing half the world toward the other direction. The sushi and ramen on board were already a good start to the weekend. I stayed at the fund manager's house in a Japanese (non-expat) residential neighborhood of Tokyo, and for the next two and a half days we ate mind-blowing sushi and went to bars and clubs in neighborhoods that seemed to come straight out of *Blade Runner*. By the end of the weekend, I was sold, not only on the job, but also on giving Tokyo a chance.

In late August 2002, I resigned from Greenhill. Unfortunately Greenhill asked me to work a good part of my notice period, and ever believing that bridges should not be burned, I fulfilled that request, thereby severely curtailing my available time for going on a holiday between jobs. Nevertheless, I squeezed in short trips to Cairo and Rio de Janeiro. On my three-day trip to Rio, I experienced the same lack of love at first sight for Rio as I had for Tokyo, in part once more due to a language barrier, as I spoke no Portuguese whatsoever. Eight years later, I would buy an apartment in Rio and consider it one of my favorite cities in the world. You can already guess that after my first impressions of Tokyo and Rio, and my later found love for those cities, I do not trust first impressions anymore. Besides the trips, I packed up the belongings in my New York apartment, and of course I gave going-away parties, one in London and one in New York, reflecting the fact that my life at that moment was truly divided between the two cities.

TOKYO, 2002-2003

I arrived in Tokyo at the beginning of October 2002. During the first week, I simply stayed at the centrally located ANA hotel, a short walk away from my new office. I thereby remained sheltered for another week from a truly local experience, as the hotel staff was English-speaking, room service was easy with an English menu and many Western dishes, and I did not have to deal with public transport to arrive in the office, nor with taxi drivers who often did not speak English. Perhaps the most Japanese touch was my hotel room's typical bidet toilet—this is basically a regular toilet with various water-spraying options to clean yourself, and even a blow-drying function. Then there was the bowing…bowing people everywhere, even construction workers when you walked past a construction site. These were just a few reminders that this place was really different.

Fortunately, the hedge fund had hired what could be described as "expat moving consultants" to each of us new employees, in order to help us with the basics of integration into local life, such as finding an apartment, opening a bank account, applying for a long-term visa, filing local taxes, and other initial tasks.

Within a week, I had found a modern apartment in Nishi-Azabu, one of Tokyo's most central neighborhoods. In a Tokyo context, I had a lot of space, and even two large terraces, and my first thought was that this space must be shared with others for the greater good, in the form of parties. Throwing a party is, of course, a great way to kick-start your social life in a new city, and it's a technique that I naturally enjoyed and would come back to in other moves. In terms of building a new social life, Tokyo had been my toughest move so far; there were virtually no natural connections between my previous cities and Tokyo, and my old technique of at least having a few personal introductions from friends to local people was pretty much useless here (at some point I actually tried asking my favorite London sushi chef for referrals, but it turned out that, while ethnically Japanese, he was actually from Brazil). I ended up building my social life in Tokyo on two main foundations. First, we were a tightly knit, small group of employees in the hedge fund and we went out together a lot to dinners and nightclubs. Each one of us at least had a handful of local contacts, so our joint network was, even initially, not insignificant. Second, for the first time ever, I tapped into my university alumni network. I discovered that the local Penn Club was, in the context of alumni clubs, relatively active, having monthly socializing drinks that were actually well attended. I went to the monthly drinks in my first month after arriving and met the core crew of the club, particular the directors, many of whom were American expats. I offered up my apartment for a party, and Randy, the president of the club at the time and a major party guy himself, did not need a lot of convincing. In addition to drawing on the Penn Club social network, we invited the hedge fund network, as well as the few other people I had independently met. The party took place only one month after I had moved and about 130 people packed into my 1,300 square foot apartment. The party was so good that we ran out of sake (and we had a lot) and I got a phone call from somebody who helped manage the building telling me in heavily accented English that there was a "concern about the number of guests in my apartment" (translating from overly polite Japanese, this probably meant I was close to getting evicted). The party even included a cultural lesson in that I learned that Japanese people show up exactly at the time that is printed on the invite. While in London, 08:00 p.m. would have meant most people showing up from maybe 09:30 p.m. onward, in Tokyo I had about thirty people I had never met on my doorstep at 08:00 p.m. while the sake was not chilled yet, the music was not connected, and I was in my bathrobe getting ready to take a shower. Still, the party was an undisputed success, including kick-starting my social life, and Randy and I decided that we needed to organize a number of sequels.

Over the remaining months of my time in Tokyo, we managed to have three more jointly organized parties, most notably a doctors and nurses costume party at my apartment (I invited the building administrator), where we took sake shots out of syringes, and a James Bond party. The latter exploded the limits of my apartment, and we held it at a local trendy restaurant owned by Japan's best-known sumo wrestler, with more than five hundred people attending, including the only ever Japanese Bond girl and various other local celebrities, and with *Vogue Japan* covering the event. Besides my own parties, I extensively immersed myself in Tokyo nightlife, which I thought to be one of the world's most varied and best at the time. Of course there were the regular bars and clubs, but Tokyo also had a few other nontraditional options. There were the huge karaoke palaces with theme rooms that I frequented a lot. The giant Jacuzzi bathtub room with its waterproof microphones was my favorite—I had stumbled on that one by accident one night, being drunk and entering the wrong room, only to find myself looking at about twenty naked Japanese, partly covered with bath foam, and trying to sing Elvis. Then there was a range of adult nightlife options that we got to know during various bachelor parties. There was the place that was set up like a movie theater and kept on showing short film clips on the screen—and during every clip, one of dozens of Japanese girls, all in the same short white dress and without underwear, sat on your lap. There was also the bar that was designed to look like a subway carriage, where again scantily clad Japanese girls roamed around and periodically the lights were switched off for a while (I was later told that, for those who prefer the real subway, there was a service that sent girls to meet you on the subway). We even discovered a huge S and M party held monthly at a major nightclub, and I could not help but check it out at least once, with one of my Italian colleagues. The two-storey club was filled with hundreds of people in all kinds of leather "clothes." Even though I had managed to dig out the only leather pants I owned, I was clearly underdressed (or overdressed?). Within minutes of entering, I felt the sharp sting of the end of a long whip on my leather-covered ass. Turning around, I saw a middle-aged but slim and toned woman in a leather leotard with bunny ears. The visible (and there were plenty) parts of her body were all covered in tattoos, meaning she was part of the *Yakuza*, the Japanese mafia. A small crowd of leather revelers formed around this scene, as mafia girl kept lashing her long whip at me. At some point I guess she was no longer satisfied with whipping my leather pants and came over to try to pull off my leather pants. A couple of other Japanese girls jumped into the fray as I was too surprised by the scene to react. When a small Japanese guy dressed in rubber tried to approach me as well, my Italian colleague rescued me, jumping in front of me, wildly waving his arms, and screaming, "Stop, stop, women only!" An entire separate book could easily be written about Tokyo expat social life.

While my social life was taking off, some other more mundane and practical parts of my life turned out to be initially more challenging, and it was mostly due to the language barrier. During the early days in Tokyo, I did not even manage to buy food. As I focused on investments in Europe, and because of the time difference, I left the office after 11:00 p.m. most days, and many normal restaurants were closed. My initial and preferred idea was to buy some healthy food in a supermarket and prepare it at home. That thought did not work out well in practice, as there were virtually no familiar products in the supermarket, all the labels were in Japanese only, and I could not even ask the shop assistants for help as they did not speak English. More than once, I thought I had bought some type of familiar food (say, spaghetti) only to open up the packaging at home and find something completely different (the spaghetti turned out to be some sort of fish jelly—at least that was my best guess). At some point, I almost caved in and bought some of the famously expensive fruit in Japanese supermarkets, such as US$50 grapes or US$100 cantaloupes. However, I held back and instead found the Trattoria, a slightly touristy Italian joint in Roppongi, Tokyo's entertainment district, which stayed open late and where I could find familiar items such as penne arrabiata on a bilingual menu.

The writing was on the wall, though—I had to learn some Japanese. Not only to buy food but also to be able to converse with taxi drivers, and to be able to have more meaningful conversations with local women than my overfrequent use of one of the only words I knew, *kawaii* ("you're cute"). I started taking biweekly Japanese lessons at the office. Spoken Japanese is actually not difficult to learn, with a very reasonable grammar. Written Japanese is very tough, with three alphabets in use, including all Chinese kanji characters, of which one apparently needs to know thousands just to be able to read the newspaper. Since I did not need Japanese for my Europe-focused work, my Japanese studies were entirely geared toward "social" use, and, while I learned some written Japanese, I focused on the spoken language. Thanks to my intense social life, I gained a level of fluency relatively quickly and it made a huge difference in my life. Simple day-to-day things that were previously a challenge, such as taking a taxi, going to the supermarket, or ordering dinner, once more became as easy as they were supposed to be. I picked up a very clear, if somewhat obvious, message: if you are in a place where English (or any other language you happen to know) is not widely used in daily life, do learn the local language—it will greatly improve the quality of your life.

    I cannot complete any discussion of Japan without briefly mentioning two other interesting experiences. One was the occasional moment of what some call "reverse racism." This was basically discrimination against non-Japanese, and particularly Caucasians. More than once I tried to flag down a taxi at night, only to have the taxi slow down enough until the driver could presumably see me, then switch off the taxi sign and speed off—always a welcome experience, particularly in times of pouring rain. A more blunt experience was the occasional nightclub bouncer telling you that a club you wanted to enter was Japanese-only. These were the most severe examples of different treatment of non-Japanese that I experienced. There were some other lighter forms in daily life. For example, many restaurants had different menus in Japanese and in English, the English ones at times having a tenth of the number of menu items. The second experience was the seemingly complete lack of crime: one could leave his or her motorbike with the key in the lock on the street while going to the office or shopping, and chances were that nothing would happen. I stopped locking my apartment door. So here were two aspects of life that I had taken completely for granted as long as I could remember—absence of racism against me and presence of crime—that were completely different in Tokyo.

Within perhaps three months of my time in Tokyo, I felt reasonably adapted. I had reached good fluency of spoken Japanese, I had a strong social network, I managed to buy food, and I had joined a gym. As a cultural side note, in the gym I had to always wear a long-sleeve T-shirt to cover up a tattoo on my arm, as tattoos in Japan are associated with the Japanese mafia. In my working world, there was not even any need for adjustment because we worked pretty much in our own small group and I only dealt with European companies. Having reached a comfort zone in terms of my daily life, I started exploring Japan and visited places including Kyoto, Okinawa, and Sapporo. Skiing in Japan was a particularly memorable experience, with bowing lift attendants greeting you at the top of each ski lift, and the main après-ski activity being hanging out in a typical Japanese *onsen* hot bathhouse. Here, outside of Tokyo, my new language skills were even more important.

I left Tokyo in April 2003 with some sadness. While I never thought I would like to permanently live there, I would have liked another year or so to explore the city more. I felt like I had not even come to the end of the initial passionate "love affair" stage of my life in the new city. Of course, we had one final, massive farewell party at my apartment, again with well over a hundred people. To this day, I remain very fond of Tokyo, Japan in general, and my experience there. The legal name of my main company in Brazil is Ichiban, meaning "number one" in Japanese and used, inter alia, as an affectionate term.

BACK TO LONDON ONCE MORE, 2003-2007

Moving back to London was rather anticlimactic, and not merely because I felt sad to leave Tokyo so early. It was the third time I arrived in London, after my initial move from New

York City in 1998, and coming back from Sydney in 2001. I knew the city, and I slotted effortlessly back into my already existing social network. In order to bring some new element to the London experience, I at least chose to move to a slightly different neighborhood than the ones where I had lived before, just as I had done when I moved to New York the second time. In London, I had already lived in Islington, Covent Garden, and Marylebone. My latest flat was in the very traditional neighborhood of Belgravia, close to Hyde Park, Sloane Square, and Harrods.

During the next three years I was almost in danger of settling down for good. Work at the hedge fund was interesting, with a lot of investment opportunities around at least until approximately 2005. I bought a house in Covent Garden and renovated it. I kept on expanding my social network in London, for example by starting a monthly get-together for Germans and German speakers, the *Stammtisch*. I even was in a steady relationship. On the back of the financial services industry, London was booming, with an ever more vibrant cultural, gastronomic, and nightlife scene. It really felt like the capital of the world in those days, the Rome of its age, having eclipsed New York in my mind.

In 2005, change came back to my life again. During the summer, I broke up with my girlfriend. Being single in a place such as London can in itself be a mind-broadening experience, as you can meet so many diverse and interesting people who can open up new perspectives for you. On the work front, as well, things happened to open my eyes to new horizons. We started having biannual off-site meetings of our fund in several international locations. The first one was in November 2005 in Moscow, then a hot emerging market. As preparation for the off-site, I analyzed various companies in Russia as investment opportunities and became rather enthralled, as I saw much more value there than in the developed European markets that I was usually covering, where investment opportunities seemed ever more difficult to find. In December 2005, I made use of an offer of my boss to spend a couple of weeks working out of the fund's Hong Kong office and once again found myself at one of the centers of a thriving emerging market. In April 2006, the second off-site of our fund took place in Beijing, giving me yet another glimpse of China. The third, in November 2006, was in Mumbai, meaning I had visited three of the four so-called BRIC countries (the acronym for Brazil, Russia, India, and China, the most significant emerging markets in the world) in less than one year. In all of these places, I was fascinated on a professional level by the investment and general business opportunities, and on a personal level by the dynamism and electrifying pace of life in these high-growth economies. These experiences raised my interest in spending more time in those countries, albeit there honestly was no explicit thought yet of moving to any of them, let alone of becoming an entrepreneur there. I just thought I would try to get more exposure to these places, probably via more investments there through the fund, presumably meaning many a business trip there for me. However, the mandate of our hedge fund limited the amount of emerging market exposure we could have to a fraction of total invested capital, and that fraction was, most of the time, naturally taken up by activities in our Hong Kong office. I hence did not manage to integrate my ever-growing interest in emerging markets into my current job, and my day-to-day continued to be exclusively focused on investments in developed Europe. While this, in the large scheme of things, was still a very interesting job, the fact that I could not pursue my newfound interest in emerging markets pushed me gently, but increasingly, to consider leaving my job.

In early 2006, I had started dating again, and it evolved quickly into a serious relationship in which we both felt comfortable enough to consider major future life plans together. Angelina, originally from New York City, was at the time my hedge fund salesperson at Lehman Brothers. She shared a similar vision of life, including that it was a big world out there full of opportunity and that life was too short to fall into a routine, even if it was a comfortable one. By late 2006, both of us were flirting with the idea of perhaps moving to an emerging market and we decided, for the first time, to take some concrete steps to at least analyze the idea, in the form of a fact-finding trip to China and Japan. Naturally, thinking about emerging markets, China would have been at the top of the list. This trip would be the first one of our research trips together. Suffice to say, we were both once more impressed by the sheer dynamism of a high-growth emerging market in comparison to our seemingly placid lives in Europe. Our flirtation with the idea of living in an emerging market only grew stronger. Meanwhile, at work, mine and Angelina's, nothing much changed, and therefore the "push" effect of wanting to leave grew incrementally stronger. By the time I got to annual bonuses, picking up another check giving me more financial flexibility, I was done with my current job. I had some final candid discussions with my boss to see whether my job could be made more interesting in some way within the fund (deep down knowing that this would not really be possible) and in the end resigned, in March 2007. When this finally happened, it had not been a minutely planned action. In fact, when I came home that night and told Angelina about what had happened, I could see a slight notion of surprise yet also envy in her expression, but mostly I could see her excitement. I think that even though we did not speak about it explicitly a lot at that moment, we both knew that she, too, would quit her job soon, and that we really would be going down the path of moving to an emerging market together. About three weeks later, Angelina resigned from Lehman Brothers (incidentally roughly around the time of the historic share price high), and our process to move kicked off in earnest, but not without a few months of time off and many trips throughout the world. All of this I will describe later, but now is a good moment to reflect on which factors of my life prepared me for taking the step of moving away from

London into the relative unknown of a yet-to-be-defined emerging market.

The first factor was simply a predisposition that I had developed for traveling the world. While my family did the early, rudimentary priming in this sense by taking me on many international trips, it was the experience of moving to and living in Philadelphia, New York City, London, Sydney, and Tokyo that eliminated any fears about things such as leaving behind friends in a place, making new ones in an unknown new city, generally adapting to life in a new city, and so on. Of course, it was also important that my trips included firsthand experience in several emerging markets, allowing me to witness the excitement of these markets on the ground. As an aside, on a purely practical note, you can imagine that along the years I had become extremely efficient at things such as packing for moves, organizing going-away parties, and figuring out life in a new city, whether it concerned social life or necessary issues such as health care. Let me be clear in that I realize that I have been privileged and lucky with regard to being able to make all these journeys and moves. However, ultimately I do not believe that you need the same experience that I had—you just need to have the disposition and the open mind.

The second factor was a catalyst that left me unsatisfied with my status quo: my increased boredom with investing in developed markets.

The third factor was that I was comfortable in making a radical shift in my life, such as a move to an emerging market. I had earned enough money to be flexible at least for some time (I do not believe you need this level of resources, but I would advise having at least a few months' buffer). I had no kids, which otherwise would have made me think whether I could burden them with the intensity of such a move. I did not have a partner locked into a local job; Angelina, my girlfriend at the time, was instead thinking along the same lines as I and was therefore naturally wholly supportive. I myself did not have a job that locked me down locally in any way.

The fourth factor, as always, was a measure of luck and serendipity, which came in many ways. For example, I just happened to have a lot of Brazilian friends in London, who would ultimately help me in my move.

All of these factors had combined in getting me to the point in which I was relatively young, free, with resources, and feeling capable of going wherever I wanted to go. But where to go?

CHAPTER 2

WHERE TO GO?

So now we "just" had to figure out where to move. I had not been in this exact situation before. The closest I had come to this type of decision is when I chose between London and Paris when evaluating options for leaving New York City, but those were just two choices, and I already knew both cities relatively well. All my other moves already came with a predefined location: Philadelphia for university, and Tokyo and Sydney (and New York and London) for work. This time it was different as the decision was ours, and only ours, and there were many potential choices. I knew that we needed to develop criteria for choosing our new home. Before I delve into explaining the very systematic way in which we did that, I cannot overemphasize exactly how exciting this feeling was at the time. At some point, I had bought a globe-shaped pillow (including a map of the world) and would often find myself lounging on my sofa in my London living room, staring at the various continents and countries on the pillow and realizing that I could go wherever I wanted. It was a feeling of pure unadulterated freedom.

When we started our analysis process, we did not have any criteria defined, but we both knew that simply saying that the destination would have to be an "emerging market" was not enough of a criterion. I did not even know what that term really meant in a hard-defined way. I am sure there must be a formal definition around, perhaps by the UN or the World Bank or the IMF, but I never bothered to try to look it up. What mattered for me was my own perception of what makes an emerging market—a marketplace that still has enormous growth potential, has the fundamentals (e.g., resources) and macroeconomic policy to exploit this potential, and, importantly, has already shown signs to do exactly that. The combination of all of these points was crucial; I certainly did not want to waste time in any place that had a lot of potential in theory but showed no signs of realizing it. While I was highly motivated to do my part to help realize this potential of whatever place I would move to, I knew that I needed a supportive environment, politically and culturally, to allow me to do so. There is an old, overused quote saying that "Brazil is the land of the future… and always will be." This certainly had been true of Brazil for many years, and it is true today for other countries. I did not want to live in a country like this. I wanted to live in one that had entered the future, that was on a visible upward trajectory, but ideally on the beginning part of that long upward trajectory. I did not feel the need to arrive in a country at its low point; I was quite happy to arrive after an initial upswing had already commenced. Stock market investing had taught me that trying to invest in things at the lowest point has typically a lower risk-adjusted return than giving up the initial 10, 20, or 30 percent of upside. So here was the first macro criterion: a place with huge growth potential that had started to realize the potential. Judging countries on this criterion was, initially, possible simply by looking at macroeconomic data. For judging the solidness and sustainability of the economic momentum, though, I found it inevitable to be on the ground in these countries, which I will talk more about later.

This first criterion still left many countries in the game. Besides the BRIC (Brazil, Russia, India, and China) countries, there were, for example, Mexico, Chile, Colombia, South Africa, various other Sub-Saharan African countries, Egypt, maybe Israel, the UAE, Qatar, Turkey, Thailand, Vietnam, Indonesia, and perhaps even Iraq. It really is a big world out there, even if it felt small and accessible in my hands in the form of a globe pillow.

The second macro criterion was that there had to be accessible opportunities present in the emerging market for me to get involved and make a difference. It's exciting simply being in a thriving emerging market, but I did not want to be merely an observer; that might be satisfactory for a short visit as a tourist or on a business trip, but not when you decide to move there. I was certain I wanted to get involved in the economic growth in some way, at the very least by working in a "regular" job, but deep down I already knew that I might end up being an entrepreneur. When I speak about "accessible opportunities," the stress is not so much on *opportunities*; in any of the markets above, these are a given, and that is why these markets are growth markets to begin with. However, depending on the market, these opportunities may not be accessible to an outsider—like me. There are several potential reasons why this accessibility may not be given in any particular market. For example, the local language might be a formidable barrier, and speaking English may not be a fully equivalent substitute if one really wants to get involved in local business, like in China or Russia. There might be very strong existing local business networks, and breaking in for an outsider is challenging (e.g., in some Asian countries, like the *guanxi* Chinese business networks). Depending on the country, its economic policies may significantly impact the quality and accessibility of business opportunities. For example, while I find South Africa an interesting location to invest in, it is even more so for local black businessmen, thanks to the government's BEE (black economic empowerment) program, which heavily supports black investment in the economy. Admittedly, so far I have looked at accessibility of opportunities merely in negative terms, looking at restraints such as language, cultural, and political barriers. Cleary we can also formulate positive factors that facilitate the access to opportunities—and by that I do not only mean the absence of any of the above restraints, even though merely that already helps significantly. Government policies incentivizing investment, and especially foreign investment, are rather helpful. For example, Brazil has an investor visa program, whereby foreigners who invest a certain minimum amount in the country gain a resident visa. Another example of a facilitating factor is an attractive tax regime. For example, the Hong Kong SAR's low income tax rate certainly makes an expat's decision to live there easier, at least if that decision is purely viewed from an economic point of view.

This gets me to the point that the two macro criteria so far—availability of business opportunities and accessibility of these opportunities—are of course very much professional criteria, or business driven, or whatever you want to call them. There is a second set of criteria, which I will loosely call "lifestyle criteria." While the professional criteria, as the name indicates, rate a location with regard to its suitability to professional objectives, lifestyle criteria rate a location with regard to everything else that holds a minimum importance to your happiness in life. What exactly qualifies to hold this "minimum importance" in life will vary from person to person, but potential issues could include the weather, personal safety, the political system, the openness of local society, the state of the environment, societal structure, presence of negative elements such as racism or sexism, general infrastructure, and culture of the place in general. The penultimate term *infrastructure* comprises a number of potential things, including access to international airports, quality of health care and schools, and so on. The last issue, culture of the place, is really meant to be a "kitchen sink" term, because it could include almost anything, ranging from local cuisine to the fact that a culture is highly observant with regard to one religion. Finally, for some, the distance to where the rest of your family lives may enter as a criterion.

Those who want to move to a new place, and have the luxury of choosing that place, should spend some up-front time thinking about which of these lifestyle criteria are important to them and conduct some research. However, I will tell you from personal experience: notwithstanding how much time you spend researching up front, there is no substitute for spending time on the ground in as many places as possible. It is the only way that you will discover what you like and do not like about a place. For example, you may not think about listing traffic as a criterion when you do your up-front brainstorming of relevant criteria, but once you spend a couple of days stuck in traffic for hours in Nairobi, or Lagos, or Teheran, you might (or might not) realize that this is something that you do not find an acceptable element of lifestyle.

Besides figuring out which lifestyle criteria matter to you, and which one matters to what extent, you should also think about how much lifestyle criteria matter in relation to professional criteria. In other words, what sort of trade-offs are you willing to accept between professional benefits and lifestyle? To illustrate this, I will give two examples, which I have both seen in acquaintances over the years. There have been several cases of investment bankers moving to Hong Kong, with explicit rationales of (1) furthering their career by doing a rotation there, and (2) building personal wealth more rapidly, as after-tax income in Hong Kong is much higher than in most other places due to Hong Kong's low income tax rate. It would be presumptuous for me to say that lifestyle criteria were irrelevant in the decision-making process of these acquaintances, but from all that I heard and otherwise sensed, they held relatively less importance. On the other extreme, I have known at least one investment banker who moved from London to Sydney, the latter being, in global comparison, an investment banking backwater, but of course it includes some lifestyle characteristics that places such as London or New York simply cannot rival, such as its beaches, and the ability to close up shop early on Fridays and go sailing in Sydney Harbour (or surfing, like I did). Again, in this case, too, it would be presumptuous for me to state that he made his decision with a disregard for professional factors, but what I sense is that lifestyle factors clearly played a prominent role.

In more general terms, what are some of the factors that can typically affect the relative weighting of professional versus lifestyle criteria? I will mention some that I have come across in my analysis. First, there is the amount of time you intend to spend in the new location. The shorter it is, the more acceptable it typically becomes to underweight lifestyle criteria in relation to professional criteria—to do a "stint" in a place to advance one's career and/or make some good money. Examples include the investment banker doing a rotation in Hong Kong, the contractor working on a one-year project in Baghdad, or, at the extreme, the oil worker in Alaska. For those who are doing or contemplating doing a move along those lines, I offer this: stay open-minded and let life surprise you. In several places, including in Tokyo and São Paulo, I have met people whose time in those cities started out as short-term, career-driven stints, but who over time became enchanted with their new cities and stayed, often changing jobs eventually, and at times marrying locals and starting families. Second, the trade-off between professional and lifestyle criteria quite simply depends on your own life situation. How important is your career? Perhaps you are semiretired or even fully retired and what you still look to do, as work or just as a hobby, can be done in a variety of locations. This is a fundamentally different situation from somebody who is still playing to get to the top of his or her profession and, depending on the profession, this ambition may only be realized in a handful of places in the world. Third (technically, a subpoint of your life situation, but I consider it important enough to break it out separately), it matters if you are contemplating the move by yourself or together with other people, most important your partner and/or kids. What might be an acceptable trade-off for you might not work for your partner. In these situations, the relative weighting of the professional and lifestyle criteria of everybody involved matters. You might relatively overweight your professional criteria, and it may be a rational choice for you to move to Hong Kong. However, perhaps for your wife it may mean giving up her job and rebuilding her social life within the confines of an expat community. I am not saying a move in this case is right or wrong; I am merely pointing out how different people may be affected in different ways and that this has to be taken into account.

One final important consideration is thinking about what happens if the move does not work out well and you are forced to return. Ask yourself: "How will that time in that place look on my CV in case I need to apply for jobs again here?" or "Will I be able to reintegrate easily in the lifestyle in my old home (or will I be so used to having a large apartment with a maid in a place like Brazil that I cannot stand the thought of living in a small apartment with no domestic help in London again)?"

So how did these various criteria stack up for Angelina and me? Professional criteria clearly still mattered to us. We were both still young—I had just turned thirty-five, and Angelina was twenty-six—and even though our previous jobs had left us in comfortable financial positions, we never considered stopping working or semiretiring. In fact, there was never even a question about taking the foot off the career gas pedal: we were both hungry, ambitious individuals and saw the move to an emerging market as a chance to further our professional lives. So, we needed a place with accessible business opportunities; this was the primary criterion. Nevertheless, lifestyle criteria still mattered to us, although I will admit to you that we did not spend a great deal of up-front research time analyzing lifestyle criteria. (The paragraph above, where I laid out examples of lifestyle criteria, was written with benefit of hindsight.) I do not even remember Angelina and I having had any explicit discussion about lifestyle criteria. I think there were simply some things that were implicitly understood, namely that we would not move to a place that was too extreme with regard to any one important lifestyle aspect—whether that meant too dangerous or too hot. What else mattered to us enough to care, we really only discovered during trips to the various places; that was part of the process and, frankly, part of the fun.

Doing research trips to places where I could potentially live was something that came naturally to me, given a lifelong passion for travel. But it also made sense to me that I would have to be on the ground to really evaluate how a place scored along the professional and lifestyle criteria. In the end, there was only so much desktop research one could do. I was also influenced by a couple of books written by Jim Rogers, George Soros's founding partner of the Quantum macro hedge fund, the fund famous for successfully betting against the pound sterling in the early 1990s. After retiring from Quantum, Rogers made a couple of journeys around the world, first on a motorbike, and then with a modified Mercedes-Benz SLK convertible. Both trips resulted in books, *Investment Biker* and *Adventure Capitalist*, and both books are basically travelogues with a heavy economic and investment analysis overlay. Rogers acutely observes the economies of all the places he visited and derives investment hypotheses based on his observations. One example is when he traveled to South Korea, perceived the growth in a demographic imbalance between female and male population, and developed the hypothesis of investing in the local contraceptive industry. However, Rogers is undoubtedly most famous for having predicted the commodities bull market that started in the early 2000s, and this prediction was directly based on the observations of an imminent surge in emerging markets demand that he made on his second trip around the world in the late 1990s. I could only ever aspire to be as good an investor or even as accomplished and perceptive a traveler as Jim Rogers, but on a small scale, I certainly wanted to emulate his way of visiting and analyzing countries. So, I decided my choice of a new place to live would be based on actual visits to these places. Unfortunately, as I did not have the same amount of time or money available as Rogers, my visits were typically limited to between five days and two weeks. In an ideal world, I would have spent more time in each place and seen it in as many situations as possible (season of year, professional versus social context, etc.). But this was not possible, so I had to do the next best thing: talk to local people and benefit from their experiences and opinions.

Angelina and I did not actually visit all the places together. In fact, on some potential places, she either believed my opinion and/or quite happily ruled them out anyway for various reasons. Specifically, I visited Dubai, India, and Russia by myself, and we visited China, Japan, Brazil, Argentina, and California together.

RUSSIA

Russia, as I already briefly mentioned, I had visited in November 2005 when the hedge fund where I worked had an off-site meeting in Moscow. I had only ever been to Moscow once before then, as a teenager in 1989 together with a friend from school. Back then, it was one of my first trips without my parents and it was a turbulent time in Moscow. While I was there, Boris Yeltsin was elected president of the Russian parliament, and the proverbial winds of change were blowing hard—it was a society in transformation. It was also a place where two teenagers could have a blast, buying Russian army uniforms on the black market, getting drunk on fifty-cent vodka tonics at the hotel bar, and getting a huge box at the Pushkin theater for about US$30. Sixteen years later, instead of Aeroflot Russian Airlines economy class, I flew in on British Airways business class, and instead of staying at a state-run hotel on the periphery of town, I was at the Kempinski, just across the river from the Red Square and the Kremlin. It was certainly still a town where boys could have fun, even if they were not teenage schoolboys anymore, but thirty-something hedge fund boys—which was a good thing, as there were certainly no fifty-cent drinks around anymore. Instead, we found that the tables at the then hottest nightclub in town, a place called First that was just meters away from our hotel, required a minimum spend of US$1,000, which at the time was on par with the five hundred pounds at London's Chinawhite club. First's parking lot was full of Hummers, Mercedes, and Range Rovers. Inside, drinks, too, were London prices, but the place was packed, and the vast majority of customers were locals. We did not even manage to get a table in the VIP area and on a couple of occasions were all but thrown out for minor things, in a sign that being a foreigner here did not seem to be an advantage and maybe was a disadvantage. Lots of the women in the club were stereotypically beautiful and clad in Western designer clothes and jewelry. I soon realized, though, that my London pick-up chat would not go very far here. Being from London, which would have been considered cool in itself in many places throughout the world at the time, was not exactly a novelty. "So have you been to London yet?" I asked a slim blonde dangling a martini glass. She replied in accented but fluent English, "Sure. I go about once a month. My favorite places are Cipriani and Tramp. How about you?" referencing what at the time were among London's most exclusive restaurants and nightclubs, respectively. By the end of the night, I still managed to leave the club with two girls, one of whom did not even speak English. She had her friend translate for me that she thought I was cute and liked me. There was not really any attempt at small talk; I felt like this girl knew what she wanted, and this was just another form of consumption for her, a lust for consumption that her designer clothes, handbag, shoes, and diamond-studded watch already demonstrated clearly enough. Because all of the bars in Moscow were closed, we simply went back to my hotel, where immediately after entering my room she just said one word that was similar enough in English for me to understand: "champanski!" After stripping away layers of Chanel and Dolce & Gabbana, I stared at what looked like a red ruby in her belly button. My colleagues teased me for the rest of the time that I had unwittingly picked up some oligarch daughter and should probably get the hell out of the country before getting shot or worse.

In general, there were blatant signs of conspicuous consumption in Moscow. Just meters away from the Red Square, I noticed a billboard for Aston Martin, something I had never seen anywhere in the world (somewhat unsurprisingly I later learned that there was one in Shanghai, too). These signs existed alongside at times crumbling infrastructure, even here in the capital, and notions of abject poverty, such as homeless people in the streets. What I did not notice yet were any obvious signs of a strongly upwardly mobile middle class, especially in comparison with my later experience in Brazil. Purely empirically, it appeared that former President Boris Yeltsin's policies had created wealth for a small upper class (most notably and infamously, the so-called oligarchs), but there had been no visible effort to lift up broader society, as there had been in Brazil, for example. This was something that bothered me, both because on a personal level I do not handle poverty well, at least when I think the situation of the poor is not somehow improving, and also because I think a broad-based society is essential for long-term economic and political stability. I had my concerns about politics as it were. With recent events (at the time) including the Yukos affair (the government effectively disowning and arresting an oligarch, allegedly because he had meddled too much in politics) and the suspected assassination of dissident Aleksander Litvinenko in London, more than a few people doubted whether Russia was a democratic society ruled by law. Then there were the political activists I kept seeing on the streets, most of them Stalinists, clad in old Soviet hammer-and-sickle flags and at times carrying pictures of Stalin. They were clearly nostalgic about the "good old times" when maybe their lives were still not very good in absolute terms, but in their minds there at least existed more equality in the society. It reminded me that economic volatility can often go hand in hand with political volatility, whether good or bad.

Meanwhile, we were not only visiting Moscow's nightclubs. This was a hedge fund off-site and, therefore, primarily a business trip. We had daily discussions about investment opportunities in Russia, but more important we also had company meetings and dinners with local businessmen. One of the companies we visited was Gazprom, the state-controlled gas giant, one of the biggest companies in the world. Gazprom's headquarters were a huge, imposing and gray complex, where we were ushered into a giant meeting room that easily fit some fifty people. Gazprom showed up with five bureaucrat-looking people to our meeting, and our questions were very carefully answered, at times only after the Gazprom people had briefly consulted among themselves in Russian. I led the discussion on behalf of the fund, but I must say that despite my best efforts I did not manage to gather much new information. That Russia had lots of oil and gas deposits we all already knew. The whole thing had a feel of old-style Soviet bureaucracy. The second company meeting was completely different. Sistema was an oligarch-led conglomerate whose crown jewel asset was a majority stake in one of Russia's mobile telecom operators. Its headquarters were as different from Gazprom's utilitarian gray complex as they could be: they were in a well-located type of city palais, whose opulent style almost seemed to want to herald the return of Russia's feudal classes. We sat down in another big meeting room, a lot smaller than the one at Gazprom, but with ceilings probably twice as high and adorned with crystal chandeliers. I later found out that Sistema's headquarters building was in fact the former German Reich prewar embassy and that in one of the other rooms the Molotov-Ribbentrop Pact had been signed. A couple of investor relations people started to answer our questions, but after a short delay, the CEO of Sistema strolled in and took over the discussion, giving lucid and intelligent answers in fluent English that were more useful than those in our prior meeting. He casually sat at the huge table in his designer suit, with a supreme air of confidence, making intense eye contact with whomever he was talking. There was no consultation with the other Sistema people at the table; there was no question who was in charge. This had nothing of the Soviet bureaucracy air of our previous meeting. Given the surroundings and the main protagonist, it felt more like being in a James Bond movie, waiting for the man across the table to offer to sell you a nuclear weapon. But these of course were clichés and unfair ones at that. Sistema was a serious company, and what stayed behind most in my memory, besides the opulent setting of the meeting, was the company's clear grasp of the mobile telephony market opportunity in Russia. Penetration of mobile phone services, and also revenue per user, were still low in Russia, giving many years of potential growth. Sistema had the resources (financial and otherwise) to exploit this opportunity: they could win license auctions and they could invest in networks and in marketing. Within a few weeks of the meeting, I bought the company's shares and eventually sold at a good profit just a few months later.

Russia clearly had business opportunities. The high raw material prices (e.g., for oil, gas, and industrial metals) meant huge export income for Russia, capital that could be, at least in theory, reinvested internally. At the same time, many products common in more developed markets still had a low penetration in Russia, such as mobile telephony but also many financial products. I had pretty big doubts, though, about how accessible these opportunities might be for somebody like me, foreign, without even any minor Russian connections. The sectors where the obvious big money was, oil and gas and mining, were heavily regulated and very capital intensive, even when looking one level further back at supplier or servicing companies. Furthermore, there quite simply seemed to exist a barrier for foreigners. Among the businesspeople I met in Russia, there was only one really successful case, which was an American who had cofounded one of the most successful investment banks in Russia. However, he had done so as a partner to a well-connected Russian. There was certainly always the option of working for some company, perhaps a local investment fund or an investment bank. However, since I did not see myself as having any long-term advantage, this would then naturally have been a limited-time option, a stint. I also wanted to move to a place where the entrepreneurial option realistically existed for me.

During my time in Moscow, I also realized that the place failed or at least was subideal with regard to several lifestyle criteria. First, I visited in November, when it was freezing cold, about minus twenty. I have no particular problem with the cold—I am an avid skier and have visited both polar regions—but the prospect of enduring this type of weather for two or three months every year was not compelling. Moscow's location does not even make it easy to escape and gain a reprieve from the city's weather (or the city in general) in another place. All the cities that one can reach with ease—St. Petersburg, the Baltic cities, Helsinki—have the same type of weather. Second, I had no affinity or love for the Russian language. I generally have no issue with languages that are considered difficult or are very different from the Indo-Germanic and Romance languages with which I am familiar; I learned Japanese during my time in Tokyo and have attempted a couple of times to learn Arabic. However, there was something about Russian that I was just not comfortable with, without my really being able to define exactly what. Third, the socioeconomic structure disturbed me. I did not like to see on a daily basis how opulent wealth and abject poverty coexisted while there seemed to be no meaningful upward mobility for the masses. Ostentatious wealth does not phase me, albeit I also do not like it a lot. It seems to be a reality of many emerging markets, where there is a lot of new wealth and many of the newly wealthy seem to view money as a novelty and engage in the type of ostentatious behavior that many in Europe or the United States (where there is a longer history of being used to wealth) would frown upon. As a friend of mine once observed: "China may be one of the only places where Aston Martin sells its cars in orange." I can also deal with poverty, even though it always hurts me to see it, as long as I can believe that the poor have a real and fair shot at improving their livelihoods. It was this last part that was critical and that I was doubtful about from what I saw in Russia. Fourth, I sensed an occasional undercurrent of xenophobia, whether this was in the seemingly lack of foreigners in the business world, the treatment we sometimes got at the nightclubs, or the outright racist comments of a couple of locals that I met.

I left Moscow with a number of interesting new experiences, excitement about some investment opportunities, a few tins of black-market caviar, but also the certainty that this was not a place where I would really want to live. I should point out, as I will for other places where I chose not to live, that Moscow is well worth a visit. It is one of the world's great cities, full of history and with amazing museums, among other things. For my purposes, though, it got crossed off the list.

INDIA

For a number of reasons, it was surprising that I traveled to India for the first time when I was thirty-four years old. It is obviously one of the most important places in the world, culturally and economically speaking. The country was English-speaking and a lot closer and a lot more accessible than many other places I had already visited. Hinduism was one of the religions that I had always found very interesting. I also loved Indian food (this might seem mundane, but I do actually consider it a credible lifestyle criterion). At some point in my twenties, though, I decided to keep India "in reserve." I was traveling so much and to so many places that I started to worry about running out of options for a meaningful honeymoon trip. In November 2006, though, our hedge fund decided to do an off-site in Mumbai, allowing me at least a glimpse at India's business capital.

    I decided to forgo traveling on British Airways and opted for a much cheaper seat on Jet Airways, India's largest private air carrier, in order to start my experience of India already on the outbound flight. I was impressed: the aircraft was brand new, the seats comfortable, the service attentive, and the Indian curry—considering it was airline food—was delicious. I touched down in Mumbai early on a weekday evening and, leaving the comfortable microcosm of Jet Airways, stepped into the mess that was Mumbai airport. As I learned over time, not all emerging economies had caught up on necessary infrastructure spend, and Mumbai airport at the time was certainly not fit to be the main gateway to the business capital of one of the most important economies in the world. One hour later I finally left behind the airport and entered into a new comfort zone, that of a chauffeured car that whisked me, along a combination of good new and terrible old expressways, to the Oberoi hotel at the heart of Mumbai's business district.

    After a quick check-in, I did not waste any time in the hotel and headed out to sample Mumbai's social life. It was the first time ever that I had decided, before the trip, to try to use an online social network (in this case, A Small World, also known simply as ASW) in order to connect with people in another city where I had no friends or acquaintances. I had posted on one of ASW's bulletin boards that I was going to Mumbai and looking for people to hang out with, and a couple of French girls, Daphne and Latifa, invited me out for dinner. I arrived at Indigo, the restaurant that Daphne had texted me, and it was a trendy modern place of the type that could have been found in New York or London, or in Moscow for that sake, only that the prices were a lot cheaper than Moscow. Daphne and Latifa were already in the middle of dinner with a group of people that included a local investment banker, a couple of kids of wealthy local families, and also a supposedly major Bollywood actor. Around midnight, we took off and took a short ride to arrive at what was supposed to be one of the trendiest nightclubs at the time. Our group had split up into different cars and by the time I arrived with the girls, Mr. Bollywood was already on the red carpet of the entrance giving an interview to a TV camera team. There was a velvet rope as there would have been for any other exclusive club in a major city, but fortunately our group was admitted without any delay. On the inside, the club, by virtue of decoration and music and general atmosphere, could as well have been located in New York or London, or Moscow. I even spotted a few familiar faces from London. There was a big investment conference starting the next day (part of the reason for the scheduling of our off-site in the first place), so it made sense that there were a few people from London around. Prices for drinks were a lot more reasonable than in Moscow and here I had no problem stepping into the VIP area, albeit that was probably because I was with Mr. Bollywood. It occurred to me then that, on our social outings in Moscow, we had never had a local with us; it had always been just us foreigners. After a couple of hours, I decided to call it a night; after all, I had to work the next day. Leaving the club, I noticed about half a dozen beggars waiting in the street, one of them a leper without the lower parts of his legs, just crawling between the Mercedes sedans and Porsches that were valet-parked in front of the club. Nobody seemed to care. My parents had warned me about the abject poverty in India; nevertheless, I found this scene difficult to stomach. There were two very distinct worlds here within meters of each other. One, inside the club, I was so familiar with that it did not matter that I was thousand of miles away from home. The other, just outside, I did not know how to handle. I just grabbed a taxi back to the Oberoi.

The next day was the first time that I saw Mumbai by daylight. My room had a panoramic seafront view of a sweeping beachfront that must have been several kilometers long. The Oberoi is located in Mumbai's financial district, which in turn is located on a peninsula, and the sweeping beachfront promenade I saw was Marine Drive, also called the Queen's Necklace (the lights along the promenade resemble a pearl necklace at night). There were two peculiar things about this view that struck me. First, there were no boats in the expanse of the Arabian Sea. When I worked in Australia, my fiftieth-floor office had a panoramic view of Sydney Harbour, and one of my favorite memories is of the masses of sailboats and other types of yachts that filled the harbor, notably starting on Friday afternoon. It was a pleasant reminder of life after work and also how Sydneysiders knew how to appreciate the natural advantages of their city. Here in Mumbai, there was just empty water, which I found depressing. I did not understand it; there were lots of people here who could afford boats. Second, there was nobody on the beach. This was a startling contrast, for example, to the similar sweeping beach of Copacabana, where nowadays I have a home. Here, on sunny days, there are thousands of revelers on the beach, suntanning, or playing volleyball or football, or running. In fairness, Mumbai has some better beaches, such as Juhu, which are located farther away from the business district. In any event, I did not dwell on the thought for too long and went out for a morning run.

Going on a run is one of my favorite ways of getting to know a city: you can get everywhere you want, and you can stop wherever you want to take a look at something interesting. You are also outside (as opposed to being in a taxi or limousine, for example) and can fully take in not only the views of the city but also its sounds and smells. I started with a leisurely run up the unexciting beach promenade but was soon bored and decided to head away from the seaside and into the guts of the peninsula, hoping that the small tourist map I had on me and my GPS watch would help me to navigate. Traffic clogged the narrow streets. The sidewalks were clogged, too, with people—not only people walking, but also a number of beggars sitting or lying on the ground, some of them lepers. All of this made my run resemble an obstacle course. I ran by Bombay University and the oval park in its front, the gothic architecture and the open park space being a welcome break from the narrow and dirty streets surrounding it. Soon thereafter, buildings bearing the signs of large firms, like Mittal and HSBC, made it clear that I had entered the main business district. Some of the high-rise office buildings looked shabby from the outside, a far cry from the glass and steel towers of American business districts. In the middle of the business district, I came across a couple of shacks and a family keeping a small herd of goats. This was certainly not Lower Manhattan or the City of London, even though the real estate was at least as expensive. I took on some further sights along my run, notably the famous Taj Mahal hotel and the Gateway of India arch that is located in front of it, and eventually found my way back to the Oberoi—my GPS had not let me down. I had not seen a single other runner along the way, but probably nobody else was crazy enough to run on the clogged sidewalks like I had; surely there must be a better running spot around, I thought.

Like Moscow, the trip to Mumbai was a hedge fund off-site, and our daily program was essentially the same, featuring a number of internal discussions as well as a few meetings with local companies, facilitated by the fact that the J.P. Morgan India conference was going on at the same time. Among the companies we met were the publicly listed Bombay Stock Exchange (BSE), the large bank ICICI, and Jet Airways, whose product I had of course already tested firsthand. The fact that I have no salient memories of these company meetings somehow speaks for itself. There were no notable details, for example, in the type of people we met, their style, their way of communicating, or the information they were passing on to us. I realized that this was because these company meetings were in a way like hundreds of other company meetings that I had already had in London, New York, or Frankfurt. The company representatives talked like us, and I do not only refer to their fluent English but also to the way in which they described their business models, strategies, growth plans, current financials, and so on. This was not a surprise, as a lot of them were effectively or literally Western trained. India's education system was a positive heritage from British Imperial times, and Indian students who managed to rise to the top among their millions and millions of peers could count on both excellent domestic institutions (such as the Indian Institute of Technology or Indian Institute of Management), as well as on having a good shot at entering elite foreign institutions such as the U.S. Ivy League universities. My own university, Penn's Wharton School, had a sizeable Indian contingent in its student body. The Indian community's Kama Sutra parties were among the biggest events on the university party schedule. Aditya Mittal, today CFO of the world's largest steelmaker, ArcelorMittal, which his family controls, was one year above me at Wharton, but he was the most prominent of a large number of Indian students. Indian alumni of Wharton include Anil Ambani, among India's, and in fact the world's, richest men, with his equally rich brother Mukesh Ambani said to be the owner of the world's most expensive residence—his own Mumbai skyscraper with an alleged cost of over US$2 billion. The Indians I had met at my dinner with Daphne and Latifa also were all Western educated. Among my colleagues at the hedge fund, there were two Indians. All of this left me wondering whether this existing strong entrenchment of Western education and Anglo-Saxon business values in India would be a positive or negative for my own potential ambitions in India. On the one hand, it facilitated my entry in this market; on the other hand, it could mean that I had little extra value to add. My gut feeling was that the latter point was relatively more important. India was full of opportunity, this was not to be disputed, but, as with Russia, I wondered how accessible these opportunities were to me. Albeit, I certainly had more Indian than Russian friends, and this at least meant that in theory it would be easier to find a potential local partner with which to enter this market.

On the social life front, our daily routine involved basically some daytime sightseeing, dinner in either a traditional Indian or a trendy restaurant, followed by drinks at a bar or nightclub. The luxuriousness of our surroundings thereby increased as the day progressed, typically starting with some relatively unmanicured neighborhood of Mumbai (such as a market) and ending up in a trendy Western-style nightclub. I still had trouble accepting the screaming contrasts and socioeconomic divides, albeit no scene remained as etched into my mind as the begging lepers on the street in front of the nightclub on the first night.

The social inequality was the lifestyle criterion that irked me by far the most. Mumbai was actually acceptable on a number of other fronts—the weather was OK, infrastructure was all right at least if you had money, it was English-speaking, India was a democracy, Hinduism was a religion that I found inherently interesting, and Mumbai was geographically well positioned between Europe, Asia, and Africa. The one other factor that unnerved me ever so slightly was the ongoing tension between the nuclear-armed neighbors India and Pakistan, and between Hindus and Muslims in general. However, I regarded a potential war between India and Pakistan as an outlier event, and I even ranked the probability of terrorist threats as lower than in New York City or London (I had just lived through the July

2005 London bombings). Little did I know that the two places in Mumbai where I spent most of my time, the Oberoi and Taj Mahal hotels, would be the two principal targets of a bloody terrorist attack just two years later, in November 2008.

I left Mumbai early on a Saturday morning, when I stepped out of the nightclub of the Taj Mahal hotel around 01:00 a.m. in order to catch a flight first to Dubai and then on to New York City, where I was registered to run in the 2006 New York City Marathon on Sunday. On the thirteen-hour flight from Dubai to New York, I had plenty of time to reflect on my experience in Mumbai. Between the unclear accessibility of professional opportunities and the various lifestyle criteria issues, in particular my difficulty to live in the middle of screaming social inequality, Mumbai seemed pretty much off the list, albeit my feelings were not as strong as about Moscow. On a less rational and more intuitive note, I also quite simply did not feel at home in Mumbai, and that was perhaps the most important observation and the only one I needed to make.

CHINA

China was always going to be the most obvious destination for me to fulfill my objective of living and working in an emerging market, the eight-hundred-pound gorilla poised to become the world's largest economy in the next decades. The metrics to illustrate China's current growth, and potential for continuing growth, do not need citing. What is perhaps more interesting is the extent to which even some people in the then economic centers of the world were already convinced of the importance of China's future role. I am not simply talking about Western investment in China but rather some much more interesting anecdotal evidence. My own Hong Kong–based boss at the time had decided to raise his daughter trilingual, in English, Italian, and Mandarin. There is simply no way around China.

HONG KONG

My first trip to "China" was on one of the journeys with my family, in the late 1980s, when we visited, among other places, what was then the British Crown Colony of Hong Kong. Even long before going, I had noticed as a child that at the time most of my toys and electronics seemed to have the "Made in Hong Kong" label. During that trip long ago, I remember how I was impressed by the hustle and bustle in its streets and the endless variety of shops offering many types of electronics and other products that I had never seen before.

I did not come back to Hong Kong until 1999, when I spent several weeks there as part of a Greenhill team advising the British telecom company Cable & Wireless on the sale of its controlling stake in Hong Kong Telecom. My return to Hong Kong was intense in every aspect. The sale of Hong Kong Telecom was by far the largest M&A transaction that the territory had ever seen, and it was relatively complex because it involved competing buyers and also minority shareholders. We all worked ridiculous hours. Even for me, being an M&A banker who grew up working ninety- to one-hundred-hour weeks in New York, I started thinking of the Hong Kong work environment as being New York on steroids. I got up for morning briefing meetings at 08:00 a.m. and was still drafting presentations or checking documents or financial models in group sessions at 03:00 a.m. I got sleep wherever and whenever I could, even if it meant sneaking away for a half-hour massage in the hotel spa in the middle of the day. Yet, as I have noticed at various points in my life, certain places with a high level of dynamism, such as Hong Kong or New York, seem to infuse you with energy, and you can keep going much longer than you would have ever thought. More often than not, after we "finished" working in the early morning hours, we would not head back to our hotels but rather go out for drinks in Lan Kwai Fong, Hong Kong Island's nightlife district. The mix of people I worked with was very international, much more so than in New York, and even more than in London: there were Americans, Brits, Indians, Russians, Germans, Frenchmen, Australians, New Zealanders, among others. Interestingly, there was only one Chinese person on the extended deal team that I remember. At least the financial services universe here appeared to be dominated by expatriates. People in business were pleasantly sharp. Most of them seemed to be on limited-time assignments, enhancing their career by a rotation in a growth market, and benefiting from low-taxed income at the same time. In return they were happy to work very long hours in a faraway place with some cultural divides. In many ways, a lot of the expats here seemed like mercenaries.

At the time, in 1999, I had no thoughts about ever moving to Hong Kong—I enjoyed London life way too much—so I was not actively monitoring any business or lifestyle criteria. I did not have any time to do so anyway; I seemed to live in a parallel universe consisting of the Mandarin Oriental hotel, where I stayed, meeting rooms of investment banks and law firms, and a handful of restaurants. Among the few experiences that registered on the lifestyle front was my new-found addiction to Chinese food, especially dim sum, or, as it is known in Hong Kong by its Cantonese name, *yum cha*. In the little time I had, I made a point of trying yum cha in various places in the city, ranging from the traditional Luk Yu teahouse to the cafeteria of Hong Kong's city hall, where waitresses pushed around carts filled with a variety of yum cha, and one chose by pointing out one's preference, trying to avoid the chicken feet (or not). On the business front, besides the internationality of the expat crowd, I noticed the sheer wealth and entrepreneurial power of the city. There was no better reminder of the "American Dream" type potential to generate wealth of this place than the building where many of our meetings took place: Cheung Kong Center, the headquarters building of Cheung Kong Holdings, a conglomerate that spans operations from property development to telecoms, includes eight listed companies, and employs over two hundred thousand people.

Its billionaire founder and chairman, Li Ka-shing, today Hong Kong's richest man and indeed one of the richest men in the world, quit school by the age of twelve, worked sixteen hours a day selling plastic goods by the age of fifteen, and started his first company by the age of twenty-two. Li Ka-shing's son, Richard Li, through one of his companies, eventually emerged as the winner of the bidding war for Hong Kong Telecom, which was the deal I was working on at the time. The Li family was just the most impressive example, though, of an entrepreneurial and commercial spirit that was evident everywhere in Hong Kong's neon-sign lit streets filled with every type of merchandise imaginable. At the time, I merely registered this as an interesting fact; as I said, I did not consciously think of myself potentially diving into this entrepreneurial whitewater.

I did not return to Hong Kong until late 2005. At that point, I spent almost two weeks working out of the hedge fund's Hong Kong office. I would like to say I had a lot of interesting new experiences and insights but, frankly, it was another "parallel universe" trip, with my staying once more in the Mandarin Oriental, working European-time-zone-induced extremely late hours in our office around the corner from the hotel, and hanging out late nights at M1NT, the Hong Kong dependence of a London members' club, which featured fingerprint ID sensors at the front door and huge tanks with baby reef shark inside. Because I was working European time zone hours, I did not arrive in the office until mid-afternoon, just as well given my nighttime outings to M1NT. I also worked out in the mornings, typically going for a run around 10:00 a.m., sometimes on Hong Kong Island's most popular running trail, Bowen Road, overlooking Hong Kong from halfway up the mountains and always filled with Tai Chi practitioners, sometimes torturing myself by running up to the Peak, Hong Kong's highest point, which involves very steep trails.

To some degree, I envied my Hong Kong colleagues at the hedge fund. They were doing the same intellectually challenging, interesting type of work that I was doing, but they actually had the opportunity to live in an emerging market, invest in emerging market companies, and enjoy various other benefits, notably a very low personal tax rate and cheap domestic help. Of the latter two, I was particularly envious of the domestic help aspect. At the time, it was still possible to almost replicate Hong Kong's advantageous tax regime if one had professional help to take advantage of legal tax loopholes in the UK. Full-time domestic help, however, was reserved for the wealthy in the UK, not only because of the salary of a domestic employee but also because full-time help really only made sense if one had a good amount of space, and space, of course, was extremely expensive in London. In Hong Kong, on the other hand, most of my colleagues lived in one to two thousand square foot apartments, most of them clinging to the slopes of Hong Kong Island above the main business district, in the so-called Mid-Levels neighborhood, where the main form of public transportation is the world's longest interconnected escalator system. My Hong Kong colleagues typically paid their full-time maids about HK$5,000 (approximately US$625) per month, a very manageable amount. In exchange, the maids took care of all housework, including cleaning, making beds, washing, ironing, sewing, cooking, and perhaps sometimes more ("What about headache money?" a maid candidate asked one of my Hong Kong colleagues in a job interview. My colleague had no idea what she meant and asked her to clarify. "Oh, when your wife has headache.") In London, I paid about sixty pounds for a weekly cleaner, who, while being tidy and fortunately also very honest, had an annoying habit of rearranging my things and claiming it improved the visual of my apartment and was then insulted when I reverted her arrangements. Because I did not use my London apartment in an abusive way, a weekly clean was entirely sufficient, and I was not really that envious of this aspect of my Hong Kong colleagues' domestic services. Outsourced washing and ironing was also replicable in London at a reasonable cost by way of the "service wash" option in local Laundromats. However, the option of having a maid who was also a good cook was a real benefit. While I was reduced to trying to find good and healthy food among London's sandwich shops, my Hong Kong colleagues had their maids cook up predefined weekly meal plans. In any event, maids were a normal part of Hong Kong lifestyle, and the sheer extent of this professional group, which is substantially made up of Filipinas, is obvious to whomever takes a stroll in Hong Kong Island's Central district on a Sunday: on this their day off, the thousands of maids meet up with each other literally on the streets of Hong Kong—as they typically save or send home most of their meager salaries, they cannot afford to meet up in coffee shops or the like. The vast majority are live-in maids, who live in small rooms inside their patrons' apartments or houses, so inviting their friends home is also not an option. Instead, they camp out picnicking on large blankets in public squares, wide street sidewalks, and any other public space they can find. It was an image that was both impressive but also for me one that conjured up slightly mixed feelings about the sometimes all-too-clear class distinctions that existed in most emerging markets—whether it was Filipino maids in Hong Kong, Indian construction workers in Dubai, or Chinese countryfolk in the huge industrial complexes of Southern China. On an admittedly purely selfish note, though, I liked the idea of having domestic help, and it seemed a welcome additional perk that I would likely have this benefit no matter to which emerging market I decided to move.

My final impression of the late 2005 trip to Hong Kong was a useful reminder of the importance of a certain lifestyle criterion for me. On one of the nights, leaving the hedge fund office, I came across thousands of Hong Kong citizens participating in a peaceful candlelight march in support of universal suffrage for Hong Kong. While the Hong Kong SAR (Special Administrative Region) of the People's

Republic of China enjoys a number of privileges and freedoms in comparison with the Chinese mainland, this is not a democracy: for the moment at least, the majority of its legislative assembly, and its "chief executive" are effectively appointed by the Chinese government. While this had never directly affected me while I was in Hong Kong (or later in mainland China), I did not like it either. I realized that I prefer democracies even in their most imperfect and turbulent, and sometimes inefficient or even violent forms, to totalitarian political systems, no matter how "well the country ran" with regard to things such as economic success or lifestyle of the majority.

My next trip to Hong Kong, in late 2006, occurred under different circumstances. By that time, Angelina and I had reached a level of mental commitment to potentially move to an emerging market that we were ready to take our first concrete action: a one-week exploratory trip to Hong Kong, Shanghai, and Tokyo. For me, it was something like my sixth trip to Hong Kong, while for Angelina it was the first time. Therefore, we did almost the full tourist program—walks in Kowloon and Central, beach time on Hong Kong Island's Southern side, Stanley Market. I even dragged Angelina to Ocean Park, Hong Kong's local amusement park, where roller coasters cling to the seaside cliffs. Angelina is a food lover like I am, so of course there was an ample sampling of the local food scene, ranging from dim sum at the old teahouses to high-end Chinese food at David (Shanghai) Tang's China Club members' restaurant. We took many of our meals in the company of locals, either contacts of Angelina or mine, in order to get locals' perspectives on life in Hong Kong. In the mornings, we went jogging on Bowen Road, and at nights we hung out in bars ranging from M1NT to dive bars such as Insomnia in Lan Kwai Fong.

There were certainly aspects of the lifestyle that we liked, including the food, the good infrastructure, and the sheer ease of slotting into the expat community. However, ultimately neither of us felt that Hong Kong could be a home. Framing it in relationship equivalents, for me Hong Kong felt like a girl I had flirted with a few times in the past, somebody who had once held a certain mystique for me, but after seeing her a few more times and getting to know her better, I realized that there was no trace of passion left, that I did not like the day-to-day routine life, and hence that I did not want a relationship. Staying in the same framework, for Angelina, Hong Kong was like the ex-girlfriend of mine that she never even started to like one bit, and did not want to have anything to do with in her life, even if there were some attractive character traits. Having been born and raised in one of the world's greatest cities, New York, and having chosen one of the other great cities as her then current home, London, Angelina's standards for a new city to call a home were very high, and Hong Kong did not cut it for her. She thought it too sterile, too segregated, too artificial of sorts (I made a mental note at that point that Dubai really would not fly for her). One particular lifestyle aspect that we both found unacceptable was the level of air pollution. Due to weather conditions at the time, clouds of pollutions had drifted down to Hong Kong from the industrial complexes farther up the Pearl River, and all of our days in Hong Kong were extremely hazy, with the sun at times being barely visible behind the cloud of smog.

As for professional criteria, we never even discussed them a lot; the conclusions seemed all too obvious. It was late 2006, the height of the bull market, and Hong Kong was the main financial hub for the world's most important emerging market; if we wanted to move there, we were both certain that we would easily find jobs in finance. At the same time, I never really considered the entrepreneurial option: China, including Hong Kong, seemed to be full of entrepreneurial opportunities if you were a local, with good connections, and speaking the language. I did not come across many examples of foreign entrepreneurs, except the occasional hedge fund manager, who used Hong Kong as a base for Pan-Asian investing but whose client/investor base was really in the West.

Fittingly, the day we left Hong Kong was the haziest of our time there. Driving by Hong Kong's giant port, we did not even manage to see the freight cranes. We commented on that fact but, besides this, did not talk further about our feelings about Hong Kong. It was not necessary. Shanghai was calling.

SHANGHAI

About two hours later, we arrived in Shanghai. Another Chinese megacity greeted us with yet another gleaming and highly efficient airport. Whatever our final conclusions about China as a potential new home, there was no denying that the infrastructure was superb. We quickly cleared passport control, flashing the Chinese visas we obtained the day before. While it was a slight nuisance that both of us, being American and German citizens, needed to get pre-departure visas, at least this was not the painful bureaucratic visa procedure that we had encountered in some other African and Asian countries. We did not have to benevolently stare at some bored custom official shuffling through papers for a long time, nor was it necessary to apply for a visa weeks in advance. In fact, it was possible to get a Chinese visa within the same day, via an "express service," for a significant extra fee—just another proof of Chinese commercial pragmatism.

We proceeded to Shanghai's version of an airport express. The Shanghai airport train is the world's only commercially operating magnetic levitation train. Sleek and futuristic, it is an impressive statement in itself of China's role as the country of the future. We accelerated quickly to about 515 kilometers per hour, seemingly flying low over the suburban countryside. I could not help thinking that this was a hell of a lot nicer than the taxicab rides, along congested highways, from Mumbai's or Moscow's airports (to be fair, it was pretty much better than any airport commute anywhere in the world). Inexplicably, our ride terminated abruptly in what can best be described as a semisuburban area of Shanghai, from where we would still need a cab ride of about twenty minutes to get to our centrally located hotel. Suddenly, London's Heathrow Express seemed to have gained the upper hand again over Shanghai's futuristic contender.

We arrived at our hotel, 88 Xintiandi, which had all the Western comfort that I was used to from high-end hotels in Moscow, Mumbai, and Hong Kong. Then we wondered what we would actually do in this city.

Shanghai was different, in many ways. As opposed to Hong Kong, it was a new city for both of us, which made it instantly more exciting, as it would be a place that we would truly explore together. I realized that I thought this an important feature for moving together as a couple. I liked this idea of exploring together—as opposed to any notion that one partner would drag along the other to a place that somehow already was "his" or "her" city.

So we set out together to explore. We went to ancient temples and rooftop bars at supermodern skyscrapers; traditional dim sum teahouses and ultrastylish lounges overlooking the Bund, Shanghai's colonial riverfront promenade; Chinese antique fairs and the best of electronics and high-end fashion shopping, including the local outlet of Anglo-Sino fashion brand Shanghai Tang. As we sipped drinks at the YongFoo Elite, a young people's private members' club in an old colonial house in a sprawling park, after half a day of Chinese antique shopping in a warehouse in Shanghai's suburbs, we were already convinced of a good part of the city's lifestyle aspects, and that is without mentioning the amazing Chinese food options we had found. The city felt like it had more edge than Hong Kong, at least from a lifestyle criteria point of view. Even the air pollution seemed better than in Hong Kong, albeit not a whole lot. I tried to go running a couple of times but did not last for more than half an hour, mostly due to the heavy traffic of vehicles, bicycles, and pedestrians everywhere.

There was a distinct lack of focus on research of the professional criteria, though, while we were in the city. And neither Angelina nor I really brought up this point at first. In the end, what had happened, though, was that the two of us had come to the same conclusion: Shanghai did not score highly on the professional criteria. It was not yet the same international financial center that Hong Kong was, and hence finding finance jobs here would be considerably more difficult. With regard to entrepreneurial perspectives, the same conclusions applied that we had come to in Hong Kong—namely, that it was a difficult proposition for non-Chinese. The type of expat job opportunity that seemed to exist aplenty in Shanghai was a job at the local operations of a large multinational. Yet those jobs were, rightly or wrongly, of no interest to us.

BEIJING

I shall talk about Beijing merely for completeness, as my trip there was not a formal research trip; I never thought about living in Beijing. Rather, I went to Beijing on another one of the hedge fund's off-sites, in April 2006, or about six months before Angelina and I took our first research trip to Asia. Nevertheless, my time in Beijing obviously left me with impressions that would later color my perspective on the prospect of living in China.

The first impression of Beijing was consistent with Hong Kong and Shanghai: a formidable, modern airport. And thanks to using a good travel agency, we were greeted by our travel agency representatives even before passport control, and they quickly ushered us through what normally was the diplomatic lane. We stepped into a bunch of waiting limousines to take the approximately half-hour ride to the Hyatt Regency hotel. My first impression along the way was the grandeur of the highway—a double carriageway with many lanes and, most impressive, landscaping and manicured flower beds on the middle strip. I could not help remembering the chaotic ride in from Mumbai airport, the rather dull commute from Moscow's Domodedovo airport, and even the Hammersmith flyover on the way from London Heathrow. Sure, this was the airport road in the capital city of the most aspiring nation on earth, and also the city in the run-up to the next Summer Olympic Games, but nevertheless this was the most impressive ride in from an airport that I could remember, seemingly sending a message that as a country, "China has arrived." The density of tinted glass-front skyscrapers and other buildings slowly increased, before arriving at the Hyatt. Inside, as in the Kempinski in Moscow, or the Oberoi in Mumbai, the surroundings were such that one could have been in any five-star hotel in any big city in the world. So staying inside, of course, was not an option.

Besides yet another investment conference, our hedge fund's off-sites always had a well-planned-out schedule of visits to key sights and good local restaurants. We grabbed a Chinese feast-like lunch, with all of us seated around a giant round table, and dozens of foods were laid out in the middle on the mandatory lazy Susan (the rotating round platform that allows every diner to turn every dish to his or her proximity). Unfortunately, I waited in vain for the style of foods that I remembered from Shanghai, as items such as abalone and sea cucumber appeared in front of me. After lunch it was off to sightseeing at the Forbidden City. While it was truly astonishing in general, the memory that stuck with me was the sudden sight of a Starbucks kiosk literally in the middle of the Forbidden City. I thought this an impressive sight even in the context of China's current economic openness and commercial pragmatism; it seemed somewhat equivalent to seeing a Mao statue on the National Mall in Washington DC (the Starbucks has since been removed). However, of course, China's openness was in the realm of commercial activity only; in politics, this was still a totalitarian country. When we stepped onto nearby Tiananmen Square, I could not help thinking about the bloody crushing of the 1989 student protests here, the images of a single unarmed protester in front of a government tank, among others. A slight shudder ran down my spine when a group of a dozen or so policemen marched by in formation, expressionless and virtually goose-stepping. It was a useful reminder of the importance that political environment held for me as a lifestyle criterion.

The Starbucks in Beijing's Forbidden City (now removed)

That night, I went to hang out with several of my colleagues in Beijing's Houhai area, a lakeside entertainment district, where a number of bars hug the lakefront. It could have been anywhere in the world. We had a good time having drinks and catching up; the fact that we were in China did not particularly enter into the conversation and, frankly, our surroundings did not give it away too much either.

The next day, we spent a lot of time at the investment conference meeting a number of large companies, from coal producers to consumer goods retailers. Everybody seemed to have the same obvious growth story to tell. And everybody was Chinese, some more apparatchik looking, some less, but always Chinese. In Moscow I had gotten to know at least one saving-grace token foreign entrepreneur; here in Beijing there was none, which reinforced my stereotype about the accessibility of the Chinese business opportunity. Even the executives from big Western firms entering the market were Chinese. In between the various similar-sounding growth stories, I slipped out for a mid-afternoon run. I set off from the Hyatt without any particular direction. After a few blocks, I felt weary and sapped of energy. The streets all seemed similar—big and lined with commercial buildings—and most of all, there was heavy smog hanging over the city, all but obscuring the disc of the sun. It all felt very gloomy. Sure, Hong Kong had pollution, too, but it also had its striking beauty, the contrast of steep mountains and skyscrapers and the sea; Beijing just seemed gloomy. In a gloomy mood myself, I aborted my run (something I almost never do) and headed back to the Hyatt. Beijing had just failed on a lifestyle criterion.

At night, we took a one-hour bus ride out to the Great Wall of China, more specifically, to a "wild part" of the wall, not manicured for tourists, not repaired and restored; here we had to carefully climb between broken stones. At sunset, on top of one of the ancient watchtowers, we had champagne out of crystal flutes; it all felt very decadent. As I reflected on the decadence and the ancient monument on which I stood, I thought of China's recurring history of opening itself to trade with the world, growing rich, experiencing internal strife between rich coastal regions and poor interior rural areas, closing itself off, finding some strong leader to reunite the country once more. I wondered whether the country would ever break this cycle, and I also wondered whether I wanted to be there to find out—but I already knew the answer then.

Another day and similar-sounding company growth stories later, we were on our last night out in Beijing. Fortunately, we had dinner at an Italian restaurant, as at that time I had somewhat overdosed on sea cucumbers. After dinner, a hard-core group of the usual suspects stuck around. Our first stop was what somebody indicated to me as Beijing's hippest club at the time, The World of Suzie Wong named after the famous literary prostitute. Suzie Wong had nothing on First in Moscow (there were no Hummers and Porsches outside, no grand entrance); instead, a dark staircase led into the club on the upper floor of an industrial-looking building. Inside, though, it was packed and great fun. We took shots of some unknown drink out of lab glasses and met some random models from Ukraine, dancing to the latest Western dance tunes. It could have been anywhere in the world, but then again, the specific mix of people, the specific atmosphere, was very unique. It felt more bohemian and alternative than the Hong Kong or Shanghai clubs, and I actually appreciated that part. Many lab glass shots later, we were ready for the next location. As always, in any place around the world, I trusted cab drivers' opinions with regard to interesting nightlife options (as long as you make it clear that you do not want to be taken to a brothel or strip club where the cab driver receives commission); however, this time we were not prepared for what was coming. After a taxi ride that seemed to take way too much time, the cab crossed a big parking lot and dropped us off in front of a big building with Cyrillic neon letters on its front. Entering the place, it really appeared that the majority of people were non-Chinese, and possibly Russian, a fact underlined by the Russian music in the background, and the prevalence of vodka bottles on the tables of the duplex, ballroom-like establishment, which looked like a huge restaurant that turned to a club at night. I like places that feel like a melting pot, so the place felt strangely compelling. There also were some very nice-looking Western girls around. I found two of them by themselves at one of the upstairs tables and struck up a conversation, only to be interrupted by one of them after two minutes with the all-time romantic phrase, "Sorry, honey, you should know that we are prostitutes." To underline the point, at the exact moment, a burly-looking Russian guy sat down at the girls' table. That was my cue to take off, and I downed a few more vodkas with the other guys. It was time to head home and to try to make the flight back to London that was scheduled to leave some four hours later. On the way out, I saw three Russians beating up some poor Chinese guy next to the DJ box. I understood that Beijing had colorful nightlife options, but it did not counterbalance my other lifestyle criteria concerns, let alone the issue about accessible business opportunities in China.

SOUTH AMERICA

Angelina and I were excited to go to Latin America. It was our first, and only, research trip that we would do together while we were not working, so we had all the time in the world. We were also, separately, each excited about one of the target destinations: Angelina about Argentina, and I about Brazil. That was based on our life histories, as Angelina had some very good memories of extensively traveling in Argentina, and I had similar memories of my several short trips to Brazil. Angelina also speaks fluent Spanish, and unfortunately I could not say the same about Portuguese at the time. We decided to spend one week each in Buenos Aires, Rio de Janeiro, and São Paulo. This time we really planned. Based in my Covent Garden apartment, and fueled by Monmouth Street Coffee espressos, Starbucks, and other local food providers, we surfed the Internet all day, finding hotels, restaurants, and, most important, local people to meet. The latter we arranged via a combination of referrals by friends and working the bulletin boards of social networks. We got a good response, and within a few days, we had almost all of our trip's dinners booked.

BUENOS AIRES, ARGENTINA

We hopped on a flight to Buenos Aires, connecting in Madrid, giving us a chance to load up on tapas during the layover. Then we went to sleep on board and woke up somewhere along southern Brazil's coastline. It was a beautiful day, and flying over Buenos Aires, we could make out many of the major landmarks, including the Nove de Julho, one of the widest streets in the world, that puts the Champs-Élysées to shame.

Stepping out of the airport, we were surprised: it was freezing cold—not Moscow-style cold, but certainly a lot colder than we had expected to find in Buenos Aires. "If I'm really gonna move continents, I don't need this type of weather," I thought to myself. We arrived in late July, or, in other words, the middle of the Southern Hemisphere winter, and Buenos Aires had just experienced its first snowfall in something like seventy years. I was about to make a negative entry in the lifestyle criteria column of my mental diary (I really hoped that one side benefit of this move would be to end up in a warmer climate, preferably close to a beach), but then I thought this was premature, and I also remembered how much I liked skiing and that there were a few skiing resorts just a short flight away from Buenos Aires. Angelina spoke in fluent Spanish to the cab driver during the entire ride into the city, which also annoyed me somehow as I could not compete with my few token words of "spring-break-in-Cancun emergency Spanish vocabulary." It made me feel like somehow we were not on an even starting ground in this country, and that did not seem to be an ideal situation for a couple making a big move like the one we were contemplating.

We finally arrived in our boutique hotel in Palermo, a bohemian neighborhood of Buenos Aires that had historically housed car repair shops before being converted into a hip location with boutique hotels, fashion shops, and restaurants. It was a great neighborhood to hang out in and stroll around. Palermo was also very international: the most common language overheard on the street those days was English, not Spanish. This fact in itself gave the place a completely different feel from, for example, Shanghai or Mumbai, but I was not sure that I liked that feel; it almost seemed at times like too much of an American enclave.

The next few days, we mostly ate and drank our way through Buenos Aires's restaurants, anything from *churrasco* to local sushi (the latter being very bad, at times even including canned tuna). Buenos Aires was dirt-cheap in the context of our London-framework minds. We had full meals in high-end restaurants, including a bottle of good local wine (Malbec was our favorite), for the equivalent of US$30 for two people. Until that time, I had only been to Buenos Aires twice before, one time in December 2005, when things were the same as on our current visit, and the other time in 1995, on a student trip, when Argentina's economy was doing well, the local currency was pegged to the U.S. dollar, and prices for virtually everything seemed exorbitant in an international context. Those days were definitely gone. Or in some ways, they appeared to have stuck around. Angelina and I were commenting on how local shop windows, clothes, even brands, appeared at times like a flashback to the 1980s and/or 1990s. To some extent, the place appeared frozen in time, perhaps trying to cling onto a glorious past that had already passed, at least for the time being. This was somewhat in keeping with the type of comment that we had heard from many foreigners, inside and outside of Argentina, that the country used to be one of the world's richest once upon a time. This, of course, was true, only that "once upon a time" was about a hundred years ago. All of this was too much nostalgia for me; I wanted to go to a forward-oriented place, not one that was perhaps desperately clinging to a bygone past. And that was exactly what, probably unfairly, I was starting to think.

This defiant ignorance of the perhaps objective current lack of forward perspective came through in some of our meetings with locals too. The local (Argentine) head of a private equity fund basically used lifestyle arguments to justify his investment focus on Argentina instead of Brazil—investment decisions driven by where the country club seemed better. The chief economist of a big investment bank provided us with some very interesting data points. However, for me, the single most impressive (and unintended) data point was when he asked us to take along his résumé when he heard that our next stop was São Paulo. On the streets, we noticed frequent demonstrations; it seemed like almost every day some demonstration was blocking off some street, forcing our taxi drivers to change routes. One demonstration we came across allegedly was by staff of the national statistics office, and allegedly one of their grievances was that the government effectively forced them to falsify key economic data, such as inflation. It would be an understatement to say that all of these impressions left me lukewarm with regard to choosing Argentina as a place to invest both significant time and money. I had this prejudice even before leaving on the trip and once or twice mentioned something to Angelina, including pointing out that the trading volume on Argentina's stock exchange at the time was about 1 percent of the volume of trading on the Brazilian exchange, and the obvious implications this held for a financial services professional such as Angelina. However, on the trip I decided to keep my mouth shut and let the impression speak for itself. I knew when not to say, "I told you so." I also certainly did not want to run the risk of triggering some emotional backlash response whereby perhaps Angelina afterward would try to find negatives in Brazil, just to get back at me.

To be fair, we had some encouraging meetings, too, specifically with entrepreneurs. The presence of a large well-educated middle class, combined with access to cheap human resources and reasonable infrastructure appeared to be a good environment to incubate entrepreneurs. Among our dinner companions were Michelle, who had a successful luxury travel company that offered customized travel experiences in Argentina and Uruguay to high-net-worth foreigners, and German, who had started Latin America's largest online hotel booking site. Now, for me, who was ready for a gearshift into entrepreneurial life anyway, the thought of developing an Internet start-up out of a chic renovated Palermo townhouse was reasonably compelling. However, Angelina's career curve had not reached the entrepreneurial stage yet, and the realistic prospects of finding a compelling finance job in Buenos Aires seemed bleak. She certainly did not want to become that person who would hand out her résumé to friends traveling to Brazil.

As an intersection between professional and lifestyle criteria, I was also quite simply almost depressed by the lack of energy and momentum in Buenos Aires, in comparison with places such as Shanghai. Argentina should have been a country of decent potential with its assets including large tracts of arable land, some raw materials, and a well-educated population. However, economic mismanagement by politicians had prevented the country from living up to its potential, and at that moment there was no inflection point in sight, no light at the end of the tunnel. Brazil, as I will elaborate, had noticeably turned a corner in recent years, but this was not the case in Argentina. As I already mentioned, when I was an investor, I was always wary of buying stocks just because they were cheap and seemed to have potential. I would always look for stocks that were cheap but had hit an inflection point, and in exchange for that comfort on the inflection point, I was willing to give up the early part of the gains. I turned to analyzing countries in somewhat the same way.

There were more interactions between professional and lifestyle criteria. Before I left on the trip to Latin America, several people had reminded me of the violent crime in Brazil and pointed out how Argentina was comparatively much safer. However, while I appreciated this current snapshot of the relative crime levels in the two countries, I always believed that many types of crime should be correlated with the economic situation. Therefore, I thought Brazil's crime situation would relatively improve—for example, as need-based crime would decrease, but also as increasing tax revenues would allow the government to deploy more resources in the fight against crime (if they chose to do so). Symmetrically, for Argentina I unfortunately expected the inverse to happen. Ironically, while nothing happened to us during our time in Brazil, it was on an early Sunday morning run in still-deserted Buenos Aires avenues that somebody tried to mug me. It was clearly just a random event, but in the context of what I had already been thinking, it of course stuck in my mind.

The political situation also unnerved me somewhat with regard to the potential that perhaps at some point, government actions could directly or indirectly devalue assets that I would bring to or buy in the country.

So in summary, Buenos Aires did not seem to have professional opportunities that worked for *both* of us, and it had a distinct lack of the energy and buzz that we so much liked in other emerging market metropolises. There were some minor lifestyle drawbacks, such as that Buenos Aires does not have good beaches in its metropolitan areas, but these things were clearly of much lesser importance. We still loved strolling in the city and its beautiful grand avenues, going to museums, and most of all, eating out cheaply in the many fabulous and chic restaurants. This was not sufficient to make Buenos Aires a viable choice in which to live. Rather, it made it something like a good destination for an occasional trip. In a European context, I thought of Buenos Aires being somewhat like Rome, a city that is great to visit but not a place in which I would live, at least while still being professionally active; I will always prefer to live in London. Buenos Aires was an especially good destination for an occasional weekend trip, if one lived three hours by flight away in São Paulo or Rio de Janeiro. This is exactly what Buenos Aires became to me after I eventually moved to Brazil.

RIO DE JANEIRO, BRAZIL

One morning, after having spent one week in Buenos Aires, we boarded a plane for the three-hour flight, crossing the Mar del Plata, Uruguay, and following Brazil's coastline up to Rio de Janeiro. Brazil was a first for Angelina but not for me. While professionally I had never really touched Brazil, except for loosely following our hedge fund's investment in a couple of Brazilian stocks, I had visited the country four times already, and Brazil and I were slowly falling in love, despite an unpromising beginning. My first time in Brazil was on a university student trip while at Penn, in spring 1994. We went to Rio, São Paulo, and Buenos Aires, on a typical Wharton nerdish trip visiting local companies. My recollections from the trip are very slim and include the visits to the supermarkets, where staff would remark price labels of all goods constantly, due to the still rampant inflation at the time. Ironically, then it was Argentina that was experiencing a boom.

In 2005 I spent one week over Christmas with a friend in Florianópolis (also known as Floripa), the capital city of the Southern Brazilian state of Santa Catarina. Floripa lies divided, one half on the Southern Brazilian mainland coast, the other half, connected via a couple of bridges, on the Santa Catarina island, where there are also some thirty beaches, many of which are known as surfing hot spots. Surfing was our main activity while staying in Floripa (never mind we had no real idea how to do it, despite my attempts in Australia). Every day my friend and I stopped by the surf school of our resort to take "lessons." I put quotation marks here because there was not much teaching going on. On the first day, our teachers gave us some basic instructions, including how to get up and how to protect your head from getting whacked by the board once you wipe out. Afterward, we were off to the lukewarm water with its rolling waves, to learn by doing, and the teachers entered the water and surfed with us. There were three Brazilian teachers. Two of the boys were about seventeen years old and the third looked like an aged hippie in his early forties, who probably had worked in the surf school since he was seventeen and never managed to quit. He virtually did not speak any English and would repeat the same three phrases all the time when we were in the water, sitting upright on our boards, waiting for a good wave: as soon as he spotted a promising wave approaching, he yelled, "Look da wave, look da wave." When the wave came closer, he moved on to his second English phrase, "Swim, swim, swim." When we finally managed to catch the wave and ride it for anything between two and ten seconds, unless we wiped out right at the beginning, we could always be sure to hear the same words as soon as we managed to stick our heads above the waterline again, "Good wave, good wave"— his third English phrase, and by far the most animated one. After early afternoon surfing, it was on to a Brazilian buffet lunch, where invariably we would load up on the Brazilian staple dish, *feijoada*, a stew of black beans and pork, accompanied by rice and *couve* (a spinach-like vegetable). We washed the food down with many *caipirinhas*, mostly passion fruit ones, and we made a few Brazilian friends who spoke some English. Fueled on caipirinhas, we typically first went shopping (one day we ended up buying loads of silver jewelry, which was the preferred and required look of hard-core Brazilian surfers at the time, and came back looking like we were part of a bad rap video) and then hit the town's bars and clubs. That is where we got to see Floripa's famously beautiful women. Southern Brazil is known for its beautiful women, many of whom are blonde, reflecting the history of German immigration to this part of Brazil. The groups of young women, blonde, tanned, with slender bodies (many of them were surfers), and often with dark eyes (the Germans mixed with other immigrants) was pretty much the main conversation topic of men, whether our surfing teachers or other foreigners. In fact, more than once, other foreigners came up to talk to us in clubs just bonding over the fact of how absurdly good looking the local girls were. I would have preferred to have actually talked to some of the girls rather than to other foreigners, but the simple reason that did not work out is that most of the girls did not speak English, and we spoke only about five words of Portuguese.

One of our days in Florianópolis was rained out so much that we did not even feel like surfing. We had a chat with the younger surfing guys who suggested that, since we were German, we should take a day road trip to the city of Blumenau, a German emigrant settlement north of Florianópolis. About one and a half hours later we arrived in a town and landscape that basically looked like I had returned to my hometown in Germany's Black Forest. As we approached Blumenau, more and more of the roadside business signs sported German names. In the city itself, there were German-style houses and road signs to the local Oktoberfest grounds. We had lunch in a traditional German restaurant and afterward killed time by trying to track down native German speakers, managing to find a couple. It was an eye-opener with regard to understanding exactly how multicultural a country Brazil is. It is one of the few true melting pot societies in the world, besides the United States and Canada.

Unbeknownst to Angelina, I had dozed off on the flight to Rio, still reminiscing about the blonde goddesses of Southern Brazil, and only woke up as we hit the tarmac at Rio's Galeão international airport, located on an island, about half an hour's drive from the city's best-known beach areas including Copacabana and Ipanema. As we left the plane and heard some announcements in Portuguese, Angelina made a comment along the lines of, "Oh great, I'm out of my comfort zone now. It's your world now." Even though I know it is a petty thing to say, I was somewhat happy that we were no longer in a foreign place where Angelina had almost full command of the local language while I had virtually none. That was just too much asymmetry for me to start a new life together as a couple. However, it was obvious from Angelina's comment that, while I basically did not speak any Portuguese and hence did not have any language advantage over her in Brazil, she still considered me to have an advantage simply due to my previous trips to Brazil. In other words, she had the same sort of concern about asymmetry.

We took a cab to our hotel and soon passed what seemed like several miles of roadside *favelas*, the Brazilian version of shantytowns. Millions of *cariocas*, the name for Rio's inhabitants, are living in favelas, with the largest ones having populations almost in the hundreds of thousands. At least in Rio the favelas are mostly brick buildings, and hence appear to be a notch above the metal sheet and cardboard shantytowns that I remembered seeing on the way in from Cape Town's airport. Rio is different from many other Brazilian cities in that the favelas are sometimes located in very close proximity to some of the city's wealthiest areas. This is due to Rio's topography. The city has many steep hills where regular construction is not permitted, but the favela dwellers do not care a lot about getting official construction permits but rather see the hills as an opportunity to live close to their jobs without having to commute from "regular" suburbs located farther away. As a result, neighborhoods such as Copacabana, Ipanema, and Leblon, which feature multimillion-dollar oceanfront apartments, all have neighboring favelas on nearby hills. This is different from São Paulo, which has less dramatic topography, and hence the good areas have been commercially built up, and favelas have been pushed to the periphery of the city, farther away from the wealthy areas (although there are exceptions). The poverty and inequality in Rio is right in your face. Like always, though, poverty as such did not bother me that much, if I had the feeling that something was being done to improve it.

In Rio, we stayed smack in the middle of the famous Ipanema beach. When it's sunny and warm, the beach is packed with locals and tourists alike, and joggers and cyclists occupy the running and cycling lane that hugs the beachfront. The day we arrived, though, it was overcast and just about seventy degrees. Fierce waves were breaking. The beach was empty, which was no surprise given that the locals, the cariocas, had a tendency to shun the beach even if there were a few clouds in the sky and/or the temperature dropped below something like eighty degrees. I was disappointed, because I knew Rio when it was sunny and at its best, and I wanted Angelina to see those lifestyle elements, which for me were some of the key selling points of the city.

So we left our Brazilian-style miniature bathing suits in the luggage for another day and set out to get some research done on the city. First stop was at the office of a real estate company set up by two American partners who bought and renovated apartments in Rio's beach area, with a target audience of American buyers, for whom they took care of all the gritty parts of the process of buying real estate in Brazil. One of the partners showed us a couple of their apartments in Ipanema and Copacabana. I asked him about his story and it turned out that he, too, had worked in finance in New York, before moving down to Brazil, partly because of a local woman, which was a common Brazil expat story at the time. I liked the fact that he had chosen to go down the entrepreneurial route, and from what I could tell from his comments, he had not encountered any insurmountable obstacles along the way and managed to set up his life in Brazil just fine. I also started to immediately like the Brazilian real estate sector. At that time, in mid-2007, these newly renovated apartments sold for something like US$400 per square foot on average (obviously depending on the location), but I knew he bought them typically for probably at most half that value. At US$200 per square foot, in one of the key cities of one of the most important emerging markets in the world, in a good location that was also supply-constrained (new build in areas such as Ipanema is almost impossible), it seemed like very good value. It was also at the time cheaper than prices in Buenos Aires, where the economy had far fewer attractive prospects and there were many more new buildings. I made a mental note about researching the real estate sector further.

Over the next few days, we met a few people who worked in Rio, from whom we were looking to glean a perspective on local life, professional and social. In this case, I had identified a couple of people through the Wharton alumni network, who both happened to work in local hedge funds, and frankly what they were telling us workwise was not very different from what we already knew from London. The fact that we talked to hedge fund people was not entirely by design. Going through the Wharton alumni network, which just happened to be the easy option in this case, there was always a good chance that one ended up with people working in finance. Furthermore, Rio, once the political and economic center of Brazil, had lost out in business to São Paulo, which had become the economic hub of Brazil, beginning with the coffee boom in the early twentieth century. Among the sectors for which Rio remained an important center were oil and gas (Petrobras, the government-controlled energy company, is headquartered here) and investment management—probably because hedge fund managers could pretty much choose where to locate themselves, and quite a few of them chose the lifestyle advantages of Rio. One of the Wharton alums was American, from California, and had randomly decided to come to Brazil a few years back, so we were particularly interested in her thoughts. The point we thought most interesting was that, while she had a very attractive job in Rio, she was considering moving back to São Paulo, as she considered that city more cosmopolitan in every aspect—more entertainment options, more culture, more open people, and so on. We also talked about the safety issue, as it was impossible not to when having a conversation about life in Brazil; it was still known to be one of the more violent societies on earth. There were the usual stories about having been robbed once, or even several times, about the occasional holdup of armed gangs of cars in one of the city's road tunnels, about an acquaintance of an acquaintance getting shot randomly (this time, in this story, getting shot in the hand—at least not so bad, relatively speaking).

It was impossible for us, though, to get a real feel for the safety situation in the city on this particular trip: we unwittingly had scheduled our Rio trip to coincide with the 2007 Pan American Games, and I had never, ever seen so much police presence in my life, not even in the few totalitarian countries I had visited over the years. Around the inland Lagoa Rodrigo de Freitas lagoon, bordering Ipanema and Leblon, and a Rio favorite for running and other forms of recreation, there appeared to be a police car every two hundred meters. I think the petty criminals had just given up and probably postponed any activity until after the Games. As for the more organized crime, this being Rio, I would not be surprised if some sort of "arrangement" had been worked out between the police and the gangs to keep things quiet during the Games. The safety situation was as atypical as the weather. I felt like we had come at the wrong time and would have to come back to get a real feel for Rio.

Rain may keep the beaches empty, but it did not stop us from going out at night. As my London Brazilians' contacts were pretty much all in São Paulo, we had relied on online social network ASW to give us a kick start of Rio social life. Coincidentally, there was a monthly ASW get-together in a bar in Ipanema just when we were visiting. We joined twenty or so people, mostly local Brazilians and some expats. Among the expats was a middle-aged Italian, who came a long time ago on a work assignment and stayed, becoming an independent travel agent. There was a German, roughly my age, who, while finishing a PhD in Germany, tried to come to Rio every few months and ultimately tried to find a way of moving to Rio permanently. He was doing a PhD in finance and had a few interesting entrepreneurial ideas for Brazil, so we ended up chatting for a while that evening. Meanwhile, entrepreneurial ideas aside, his short-term interests were a lot more stereotypically expat-like, as he pretty much hit on every attractive girl in the group. I could soon tell that Angelina was not particularly thrilled with my new buddy. This was also her first time of being in the environment that many female expats fear in Brazil—surrounded by stunning Brazilian women (I thought the most attractive girl that night happened to be Uruguayan, but that did nothing to calm Angelina down). We went on that night to dance for hours at a nightclub in Ipanema, where we were having many bottles of vodka, whiskey, and champagne at our table until about three in the morning, just as we would in London or New York. However, the seed of our first Brazil and moving-related relationship fight had already been sown.

The next day we had a heated discussion about how the environment in Brazil could feel threatening to a foreign woman. Angelina had heard the (true) stories of married couples moving to Brazil for work and getting divorced within one or two years. She started talking about Argentina again, where she simply seemed to feel more comfortable, never mind the worse work prospects. I thought that somewhat ironic given that Argentine women were on average not exactly unattractive either. I tried to be reasonable and reviewed with her once more why we had decided that Argentina was not a good option economically, but we were in the middle of an emotional fight, and at some point emotions also become legitimate reasons after all. Finally I somewhat snapped and said that even if we were to base ourselves in Buenos Aires, I for one would likely do something entrepreneurial in Brazil and hence end up traveling there all the time, and she would feel even worse with me traveling, without her, to Brazil. That brilliantly "reasoned" argument of mine bought me another day or so of emotional relationship stress.

Angelina did not even know, nor should she have known, given the mood that there was already between us at the time, that there was a different kind of "emotional conflict" with regard to Rio for me. A few years earlier, I had had a brief but passionate and intense love affair with a girl in Rio, while spending my winter holidays there. Given the long distance—I still lived in London at the time—no real relationship ever developed, but I had kept some very strong and positive memories, which for me were permanently interwoven with Rio. I started realizing that I was thinking a lot about that affair while I was in Rio with Angelina. To some extent I think it made me see the city with rose-colored glasses. It is in theory easy to say that one has to separate such pre-existing feelings from the decision to move to a city, but in practice it is not that simple, precisely because it is a matter of emotions.

In the end, we postponed making a decision on Rio for a number of reasons. First, there were all the atypical circumstances, such as the bad weather and the unusually good security situation. Second, Rio simply did not feel like love at first sight for Angelina (or love at third sight for me). I could see myself being based as an entrepreneur in Rio, but Angelina was justifiably worried about the limited opportunities. Sure, she could always work in a hedge fund, but in case she wanted to stay working in an investment bank, there were really no more options left in Rio. At least we both knew already that we were a lot more convinced about the opportunities in Brazil than in Argentina.

SÃO PAULO, BRAZIL

One late afternoon, we boarded that terribly convenient thirty-five-minute air shuttle, which I had already mentioned, to get from Rio to São Paulo ("SP"). Given the limited space in both cities, the two inner-city airports each have one of the shortest commercial runways in the world, which makes landing a somewhat uneasy experience at times, a little bit what landing on an aircraft carrier must be like, as the planes hit the tarmac and seem to break like there is no tomorrow in order to avoid overshooting the end of the runway down a steep hill (São Paulo) or into the bay (Rio). Just a few days before we arrived in SP, one air shuttle landing in SP's inner city Congonhas airport skidded past the end of the runway in rainy weather, down the hill, and into a gas station, killing all 187 on board and an additional twelve people on the ground.

In comparison to Rio, SP was essentially a new city to me. I had been there once before, on the Wharton spring break trip in 1995, but my only recollections were of a dinner at a typical Brazilian steakhouse, and partying at the Limelight nightclub, which like the Limelights in New York and London, was located in a church. A Brazilian steakhouse Angelina and I had already had dinner at in Rio, and Limelight was long gone, so it was on to new experiences.

We arrived in the city at dusk and both from the plane and later from the taxi could see the seemingly endless urban expanse, a sprawling forest of high-rise buildings, now with more and more sparkling lights set against a darkening sky. It reminded me a lot of Tokyo, and I thought of it as beautiful. Angelina, a born and bred Manhattanite, must have thought so too. I had a very positive gut feel about getting to know this city.

As opposed to Rio, I had no knowledge of the SP hotel scene, so we had followed recommendations on the ASW social network and chosen the Emiliano hotel. We pulled up in front of what looked like a retrofit of a former apartment block, a sleek mirrored tower with an oversized helipad on top (SP has one of the largest helicopter fleets of any city in the world, although stories that many people only commute by helicopter are wildly exaggerated). On entering, though, we felt like we had stepped into a *Wallpaper* cover—there was designer furniture and smiling, attractive staff in gray uniforms. One of the smiling, attractive reception girls poured us welcome glasses of champagne. This was a lot more stylish than the chain hotel that we had stayed at in Rio, and I could see from the grin on Angelina's face that she was noticeably happier here already.

For setting up our meetings with locals in SP, we had relied on the twin sources of my London Brazilian contacts and Angelina's networking on the social networks. On our first night, we met up with friends of one of my good Brazilian friends from London. Our host for the night was the scion of a Brazilian billionaire family. Yet he was also a serious entrepreneur, who, refusing to just live off his family's wealth, was building a financial services firm. That night he and his wife took us to dinner at one of SP's best Brazilian restaurants, Brasil a Gosto, along with another local couple, who worked in stock brokerage and travel. Everybody conversed with ease in English on a wide range of subjects, was well traveled, and just in general quite cosmopolitan. On this superficial level, the dinner could have been in London or New York. After dinner, we stopped at our host's high-rise apartment in a sleek new apartment block located in one of the city's top-end neighborhoods, Vila Nova Conceição. The apartment felt like another *Wallpaper* ambience, and the large window front of his living area overlooked the dark green expanse of SP's main park, with the high-rise skyline of Paulista Avenue, one of SP's business districts, in the background, including a huge antenna lit up in rainbow colors, a work of local artist Antonio Peticov. This nighttime view was pure Manhattan, or Hong Kong, or Tokyo—in any event, it was something that Angelina and I knew and liked. It is funny, I thought, how notwithstanding all craving for something exotic, we appreciate the touch of the familiar.

Our host changed while we had a quick glass of champagne. Then we all went to Disco, a local nightclub designed by top Brazilian architect Isay Weinfeld. Disco was packed on this Wednesday night, with groups having bottles of whiskey and champagne at the tables. We finally fell into bed around four in the morning. Between the Emiliano, the Brazilian restaurant, the apartment, and Disco, SP had certainly given us an impressive first night out.

The next morning we skipped breakfast in the hotel and instead tried out the coffee shop across the street. It had almost a European flair to it, serving a range of gourmet coffees on a canopied veranda as well as in its spacious and modern yet cozy interior. I could see myself spending a lot of time here, and sure enough I soon did. This coffee shop, Santo Grão, known and beloved by both foreigners and locals in SP, became to me somewhat what Monk's Café was to the characters on *Seinfeld*—a place where I worked, gossiped with friends, and went on first dates.

Soon after breakfast, Angelina and I discovered an important lifestyle element in SP: Ibirapuera Park, the very same park that we had overlooked from our friends' apartment the night before. While this is just one of many parks in the city, it is the most centrally located and best known one—SP's answer to New York's Central Park or London's Hyde Park. There are paved roads for running and cycling, many dirt trails, some ponds, and even a concert auditorium and a couple of museums/exhibition spaces, and all were just a few minutes from our hotel. It was a nice day, and Ibirapuera was packed with people running, cycling, or simply strolling. It really did feel like Central Park, just with a lot more palm trees, and a lot more vendors of healthy coconut water.

Besides Ibirapuera and other public parks, SP makes up for its lack of proper beaches by a number of what can best be described as inner-city country clubs: typically the size of several city blocks and often centrally located, these members-only clubs have pools, gyms, tennis courts, restaurants, and a number of other amenities. There are a couple of high-end ones within minutes of the Emiliano. We also got to know the most prominent local golf country club, located a mere twenty-minute drive from our hotel if (a big if) the traffic was not too bad, but we were told right away that this relatively small club would be difficult to get into and, even if successful in applying, the joining fee would probably run into the hundreds of thousands of dollars. Fortunately, neither Angelina nor I cared that much about golf. In any event, with regard to an access to sports-type lifestyle criterion, SP easily ticked the box for us. There also was not a pollution problem, albeit ironically quite a few locals thought so. We told them to go take a holiday in China.

Never mind all of our London referral contacts—we still ended up going to a social network get-together in SP. Here, it was slightly bigger than in Rio, with about thirty people, and there were considerably more expats. The Brazilians worked in a large variety of fields, anything from fashion to finance, some being employees, some entrepreneurs. The expats were mostly people who had come here on limited-time company assignments, with a very significant contingent of management consultants, and also some lawyers. There was not anybody yet who had exactly done what we were contemplating to do—to simply move down here outside of the context of a prearranged job. Yet this did not discourage us; all the people we met had good jobs, the economic environment was clearly good, and there were a number of foreigners who seemed to have had effortlessly settled into SP life.

The favorable economic situation was plainly visible to us every day. Our hotel was located on Rua Oscar Freire, São Paulo's most fashionable shopping street, which, while not having the optical grandeur of London's Bond Street, New York's Fifth Avenue, or Tokyo's Omotesando, still has all the requisite brand-name shops and is packed with shoppers, especially on weekend days. We also checked out a few malls, which were equally well visited. Finally, we went to the locally famous Daslu, a large high-end department store housed in a R$200 million, two hundred thousand square foot purpose-built, neoclassical multi-storey building with its own helipad, that also houses several restaurants and the local branch of Buddha Bar. Daslu makes London's Harrods look like an outdated tourist attraction. Inside Daslu, one finds mostly imported luxury brands, whose local prices are, thanks to import taxes, often three times as high as in Europe or the United States. In other words, if one came to do some serious clothes shopping, it would usually be cheaper to buy a flight to Miami and do the shopping there. Then again, a good part of Daslu's core client group is not exactly price sensitive. Then there was the already infamous SP traffic—an ever-increasing number of new cars clogged up the city's main streets ever more. In a later meeting during that week, with the Brazilian chief economist of a big bank (arranged by one of the résumé-toting Argentines), he confirmed what we plainly saw in the streets and malls: that growth in domestic consumption, mostly by a rapidly expanding middle class, was the most important driver of GDP growth, more so than exports of raw materials, which was what at least at the time many people outside Brazil would have guessed to be the key driver. A few meetings in investment banks, and with a couple of headhunters, rounded out our schedule and were also confirmatory: the economic scenario was good, opportunities were there, and they should be accessible. In other words, one should be able to find work, even if there were some details to be sorted out, like obtaining a work visa.

On the lifestyle and social front, we heard about and were offered a myriad of other entertainment options, ranging from high-end classical concerts to football games. Given that we only had one week in the city, we hardly managed to scratch the surface. Probably the most memorable additional social activity we managed to pack in was a late-night visit to the city's Japanese district, where we sang the night away in a fantastically tacky karaoke bar, featuring plastic sake boxes and illuminated waterfall pictures on the walls, albeit unfortunately no giant bathtub theme room. For lovers of karaoke and Japanese culture in general, like me, that was an important random experience in terms of making me feel at home. I should point out exactly how multicultural SP is: thanks to workers, many of whom came over during the coffee boom years, SP has the largest Japanese community outside of Japan; it also is allegedly the largest German industrial city in the world by output. Other big immigrant groups include Portuguese, Italians, and Lebanese. The city also has a vibrant Jewish community. It is a melting pot city, just like New York.

And this was probably one of the key conclusions for us: in many aspects, SP was like New York. Correspondingly, Rio was more like Miami, a great place with some business and social life options, but much more limited, and hence more suitable to occasional visits rather than to permanent life. Angelina was a New Yorker. I had lived in New York twice and adored the city. So being able to, at least to some extent, think of SP like New York was a good thing. Again I thought, for all of the desire to put yourself out of the comfort zone and do something truly exotic, I think it is a human tendency to try to find some familiarity and continuity.

On the morning of the penultimate day of our visit to SP, Angelina and I crossed the street in front of the hotel, like every morning, to have breakfast at the Santo Grão coffee shop. We arrived very early that morning and Santo Grão had not opened yet. Not knowing where else to go (or, more accurately, not wanting to go anywhere else), we sat down on a couple of chairs that the coffee shop staff had left outside to block the entrance to the veranda in order to wait the fifteen minutes until its opening time. It was another beautiful sunny day. Angelina and I were sitting side by side and staring back at the Emiliano with its oversized helipad. I had a feeling of contentedness given all the fun and interesting experiences we had had in SP over the previous days. Suddenly

Angelina asked, "So what are we going to do? Where will we move to?" I sat up. Now, that was a legitimate question, as this, our last research trip, was drawing to an end. We had exchanged our opinions on the various cities, and its professional and lifestyle factors, all along. Besides, we knew each other very well, and it was not even necessary to explicitly talk all the time to know what the other one was thinking. For all those reasons, I think, at that moment, we did not delve into any prolonged analytical discussion. Without thinking too much, I simply blurted out something like, "Well, I guess we'll move to São Paulo." I would have never said that, or at least not so unqualified, if I had not been sure that Angelina was not thinking the same anyway. "Wow, so this is it," she simply replied. And this was it. Decision taken. I had never been shy about taking decisions when it was time to take them. Santo Grão opened, we had cappuccinos and omelettes, and we went on to the next decision. No, not about what field we would work in, or where we would live, or when we would move, or the like. We knew there would be ample time to analyze and answer all of those questions. Now we felt that we needed a real holiday, especially since the weather on the beach in Rio had been so bad. We needed to decide where we could go to the beach for a week and lie in the sun. We booked flights to Cabo the same day.

THE BRAZILIAN DREAM

Before moving on, I feel it is appropriate to write a bit about why I chose Brazil.

I think Brazil's potential is enormous. The country is blessed with many of the things that the world needs today and will continue to need in the next decades, including raw materials such as oil and iron ore, vast tracts of arable land, huge amounts of freshwater reserves, and, perhaps most important, its relatively young and diverse population of almost 200 million people. Now, with prudent macroeconomic policies, and a solid democratic political system, the country is finally leaving behind the old stereotype of "forever being the country of the future" in order to become the country of the present. The country had made a peaceful transition from military dictatorship to democracy in 1985. After rocky initial years, especially with regard to the economy (I myself had seen the hyperinflation when I visited in the 1990s), Fernando Henrique Cardoso (known as "FHC") managed to successfully tame inflation by first developing the so-called "Real Plan" as the country's finance minister, and later continuing to implement it during his two terms as president of the Republic. His successor was Luiz Inácio Lula da Silva, known worldwide by his chosen nickname "Lula" and for being the most popular politician on earth by approval ratings, at least outside of totalitarian countries. Lula, from poor circumstances and without any formal higher education, became a metal worker, trade unionist, activist against the dictatorship, and cofounder of Brazil's governing workers' party (Partido Trabalhista). He lost three presidential elections until he finally won in 2002. By that time, he had fortunately transformed himself from a somewhat dogmatic socialist (more akin to Hugo Chavez or Evo Morales) into something of a pragmatic social democrat, more like a Tony Blair, including the capability of controlling more radical elements within his party. Lula continued FHC's successful economic policies and further refined social programs that would ultimately pull many millions out of poverty, and into a rising middle class, fueling consumption growth.

Brazil's moment, its enormous potential, my own immigration—all of this reminds me of a similar moment in the history of another great country. In 1931 (or, interestingly, during the Great Depression), the American historian James Truslow Adams coined the famous expression the "American Dream," which originally was the concept that any person had the ability to achieve a better life and happiness, based only on his or her own capabilities, and independent of factors such as social class, race, religion, and so on. Over the years, the original American Dream got distorted and ended up standing for more mundane things, like prosperity, fame, or even signifying for some simply the dream of having one's own home. These banalities corrupted the original concept, and, among other things, in my opinion led to some of the disastrous events that we have witnessed in America's most recent economic history. Even worse is that, according to an article in *Vanity Fair* in April 2010, many Americans now say that they have lost faith in the American Dream. Yet the original American Dream was the noblest of concepts.

I believe that today there exists a "Brazilian Dream." In Brazil, I saw this sort of excitement and motivation to build a better life and achieve happiness all around me, in all regions, in all social classes. And the statistics show it too: in a 2008 study of the Global Entrepreneurship Monitor (GEM), Brazil ranked third globally among countries with the largest number of young entrepreneurs. I have seen examples of entrepreneurs with virtually no formal education who started as courier boys or street vendors and built multimillion-dollar businesses. Lula's own story, of course, is a dream story, and an inspiration of sorts. Finally, like what happened in the United States, people are now starting to pour in from abroad, bringing with them expertise, capital, and motivation. Of course, there had been many immigrants already in Brazil's history, and many of them have made a difference in the country. In 2011 Dilma Rousseff, daughter of a Bulgarian immigrant, was inaugurated as the country's first female president, succeeding Lula. It cannot be overstated how this type of immigration is helped by the Brazilian people: I cannot think of any other place in the world where I had been welcomed so warmly and helped so much by the locals when I arrived.

I myself have become part of this dream, coming to Brazil and opening a new company, about which I will talk further on. I am also ever hiring more people and thereby, I hope, helping to realize the dreams of some of my employees too. Whether I will succeed or fail is, in the macro context, irrelevant. The point is that the country has moved beyond a certain inflection point and gained a momentum that I believe is difficult to stop. At this point, I believe, Brazil will not look back to the past, except to learn from it. Brazil's potential will finally be realized by the masses of inspired people with dreams, entrepreneurs and those who help them, and whose combined force and impact is far stronger than that which any government could ever have. Thus I believe that just as the American Dream helped to propel the United States into becoming a powerhouse, today's Brazilian Dream will help Brazil to realize its potential.

Of course, one can point out the many problems that Brazil still faces, among them continuing social inequality, violent crime, and corruption. These cannot be denied. Interestingly, if one looks back about a hundred years at the history of the United States, that country, too, still had many issues. Today, Rio is still a city where organized crime gangs dealing drugs control entire city neighborhoods and pay off some corrupt politicians and members of the police. The same could be said for Chicago less than a hundred years ago. One should also remember that the Brazilian democracy, in its latest incarnation, is merely some twenty-five years old. As time frames for countries go, Brazil is perhaps in its adolescence, and like all adolescents, it is having some problems, but it is a very promising adolescent.

In the end, I believe that the intrinsic optimism and energy of the Brazilian people will help Brazil to overcome the challenges, and to turn the dream into reality.

Competing in the North Pole Marathon

CHAPTER 3

INTERLUDE – TAKE SOME TIME OFF!

This is a fitting moment to have a flashback to that spring evening in 2007 when I told Angelina that I had just resigned from my hedge fund analyst position. While this book is principally about the process of moving to an emerging market, at that very moment, that was not all that was on our minds. The potential and excitement we felt was bigger than just the perspective of making that move. I knew and thought, and I could see in Angelina's face that she knew and thought too, that in a way we were about to face a blank slate on which we could scribble and draw some of our life's dreams.

Once we were released from the golden handcuffs of our jobs, Angelina and I knew we would be in a position of extraordinary freedom. We were both young and healthy, with decent amounts of savings from years of work in financial services, and we had no responsibilities tying us down. We did not have any kids—not even any pets. Timewise, moneywise, and in any other sense, we could do pretty much whatever we wanted (within the limits of law and ethics, naturally).

That night, we went to have a boozy dinner at a French brasserie near London's Smithfield Market. I did not stop talking, coming up with ever new ideas of potential experiences in the world, from running with the bulls in Pamplona to off-piste skiing down active volcanoes on Russia's far eastern Kamchatka Peninsula. Angelina just listened and called me "rambunctious" at some point, but it was clear how excited she was too. We could do anything we wanted with that sudden gift of a period of freedom in our lives, but it was amply clear that both of us just loved to travel.

The idea was that both of us would come up with at least one destination and the other one had to go along with it, unless it was completely unreasonable. However, I still got away with one "completely unreasonable" (at least in Angelina's view) option. After all, Angelina would still need a few weeks to wrap things up and quit her job, so I could use that time to go on a completely unreasonable trip by myself. I did not have to think too much about the destination. It was mid-March, and every April, my friend, the Irish ultrarunner Richard Donovan, organizes the North Pole Marathon, which is exactly what its name says, a forty-two-kilometer run on the arctic ice near the exact geographic North Pole. And so, in early April 2007, I left to go as far north as is possible on a commercial flight, to the former mining town of Longyearbyen on the archipelago of Svalbard, seventy-eight degrees north and solidly in the Arctic Circle. There I met about forty other runners, who came from all over the world and with all sorts of backgrounds, ranging from serious runners, such as the captain of the Irish international running team, to a self-made sixty-something-year-old Korean American entrepreneur who had climbed Everest the previous year, to an adventurous Brit who had crossed Tibet on bike and written a book about it. It was refreshing and inspiring to see this diverse, highly motivated group that contained very few people from financial services, my usual world until then. I spent the next couple of days doing a few training runs and going on snowmobile tours to Svalbard's untouched interior, where we saw ghost towns from the mining era and reindeer, and managed to avoid encounters with the island's three thousand unpredictable polar bears. Then one day we finally took off on a Russian chartered special aircraft to make the two-and-a-half-hour flight to the Russian North Pole camp, where we stayed in big group tents. After some sleep, at about 03:30 a.m. Norwegian time (albeit time zones are irrelevant at the North Pole) and in brilliant twenty-four-hour daylight, race director Richard woke us up to start the race, as he judged the weather conditions to be favorable, and one never knew how long that would last. When the starting gun went off, the forty-odd of us—all in snowshoes, various layers of special clothes, and ski masks—set off running, cheering, and jumping like little kids. I completed the ten laps of the four-point-two-kilometer circular course in about five hours and twenty-seven minutes, placing me thirteenth in the field, and more than two hours slower than my regular marathon time. For some reason, probably because I was in that "rambunctious" and slightly crazy state of mind in general, I decided that I should cross the finish line stark naked. In the minus thirty-five temperature, even the few minutes of that experience got me frostbite on nine of my toes and lots of worried thoughts about other body parts.

The top runner (Irish running team captain) finished the race in three and a half hours, while the slowest participants, walking the course, needed over ten hours. All of us were tired like hell, but we all headed to the camp's smoothed snow runway, where William Tan from Singapore forced his wheelchair through the snow to complete a marathon distance, eventually in over twenty-one hours. We all took turns walking with William to talk to him and keep him motivated. When he crossed the finish line, we were again all cheering. As I looked around, I realized that, while we were all from different backgrounds, the one thing we had in common was that we were a subset of people who were not afraid or ashamed to live their dreams, no matter how oddball and/or futile they seemed. That I found inspiring. In financial services, it is sometimes hard to forget that life can hold dreams other than just working on the biggest deal or getting the next promotion.

There was one more thought on my mind while I was taking walks over the beautifully irregular packed ice formations in the brilliant sun. Six years earlier, I had been in a somewhat similar camp in the interior of Antarctica, together with Richard Donovan, Dean Karnazes (who has since become one of the world's most famous ultrarunners, thanks to his bestseller, *Ultramarathon Man*), and three others who on that occasion wanted to become the first people in history to run a marathon at the South Pole. The weather conditions in Antarctica are often even worse than those in the Arctic, and we got delayed at base camp for more than two weeks. At that point, I had decided to fly back to "mainland" (i.e., Southern Chile) and on to London, as I was worried I would lose my investment banking job. I never forgave myself for that decision. I chose a random job, the like of which I would have found again, over a dream. Being one of a few people in the world to have run at the North Pole was not on the same level as being part of the first group ever to run at the South Pole, but at least I somehow felt that finally my priorities were moving in the right direction.

By the time I got back to London (with frostbitten toes, a medal, and a whole new level of life energy), Angelina was also a free person and we were ready to start planning trips. My Covent Garden home was just a short walk away from Stanfords, possibly the largest travel bookstore in the world, and we spent a lot of time there reading, and sometimes actually buying, travel guides. We did not only consult books though. We also got into watching movies in order to gain insights about our potential destinations, and so we ended up having lots of movie nights in, watching films like *City of God* (about favela life in Brazil), *Seven Years in Tibet*, *Hotel Rwanda* (about the genocide), and a few others. Later on, we got into checking out local music too. Angelina tolerated my Brazilian carnival CDs, but I ended up really testing her patience with the *Tibetan Incantations* album, featuring, among other items, a twenty-minute track called "Om Mani Padme Hum" with the lyrics consisting of exactly and exclusively those four words repeated over and over again.

So what were the trips we eventually decided on?

My choice was trekking in the Himalayas, in Nepal and Bhutan. We spent almost a month in the region, actually starting in Bangkok as a convenient hub, and squeezing in a couple of days in Cambodia, in Angkor Wat and Phnom Penh. In Nepal we trekked the Khumbu Valley up to Everest base camp. In Bhutan, we visited ancient fortresses and monasteries, and attended local archery competitions.

Angelina's choice was a safari in Tanzania, in the Ngorongoro Crater and the Serengeti, where we stayed in a specially set-up tented camp and were lucky enough to see the wildebeest crossing of the local river, one of the big events of the animal world.

We also spent a week in California, a little bit to review it as a long-shot option for a place to live, but mostly to taste wines in Napa and to drive a Mustang convertible down Highway 1 to Los Angeles.

As one can imagine, there are countless stories from these six months of trips, enough to fill a book by themselves. Yet of course this book right here is about the decision and process of moving to an emerging market, not a general travelogue, so it would not be right to delve into too many details on the trips. However, I chose to include this chapter because there are some general worthwhile points to take away, some of which I have already started to make.

First, as I said, if you are given the kind of interval of freedom that we were granted, you should take advantage of this privilege to fulfill some of your dreams. If you are still unsure, reread the quote at the beginning of this book.

Second, if you travel (or, indeed just go through your life) with your eyes and heart open, you will find inspiration in many places where you had never looked before and probably never thought to look. The North Pole marathon and its participants were inspiring. But I was also inspired a lot by the stories surrounding Everest, many of which I read while we were trekking up to its base camp, like Jon Krakauer's *Into thin Air* and Jamling Norgay's *Touching My Father's Soul*, the latter giving a more local perspective on Everest as it was written by the son of Tenzing Norgay, the Sherpa who was one of the first two people to successfully climb Everest. I particularly liked the story of George Mallory and Sandy Irvine, two Brits who were trying to climb Everest in the 1920s and were for the last time ever seen when they were some eight hundred feet below the summit in 1924. Mallory's frozen body was eventually found in 1998 by American high-altitude mountaineer Conrad Anker. The story of Mallory and Irvine is full of intrigue. The only personal item missing on Mallory's body was the photograph of his wife, Ruth, which he had promised to leave on the summit if he managed to reach it. We will never know whether they made it to the summit, but it does not matter. Mallory was the prototype of somebody following his dream "for the sake of it" and inspired many. He also left us with what is his best-known quote, and probably the best one-line justification of pursuing any seemingly pointless dream, in his case climbing Everest: "because it's there." In fact, I liked the Mallory story so much that I ended up cofinancing a small part of a documentary movie about it, appropriately called *The Wildest Dream*. The movie team was filming on the north side of the mountain while Angelina and I were trekking up the south side.

INTERLUDE–TAKE SOME TIME OFF!

Everest was not the only source of inspiring stories on our travels. While driving down Highway 1 in California, we stopped at the Silicon Valley headquarters of Tesla, a start-up U.S. car company. Tesla, started by a fellow Wharton graduate, is barely a decade old, chose to focus on the virtually written-off electric car segment, and in 2010 became the first U.S. car company to go public in more than fifty years.

Besides inspiring stories like Mallory's and Tesla's, I also happened to find various instances of indirect inspiration to live my life, via repeated reminders of its fragility and impermanence. Everest has a statistical death rate of slightly more than 3 percent for those who continue above base camp, and we witnessed a helicopter ferrying back the body of a fallen climber to the local Tengboche monastery for burial. Back in Kathmandu, I was sitting on the banks of the Bagmati River, by the Hindu Pashupatinath Temple, where relatives burn the bodies of their deceased loved ones night and day. In a much more somber environment, at the infamous Chung Ek Killing Fields, many thousands were killed during the 1970s Cambodian genocide, and we could see bone fragments piercing through the unmanicured earth in many spots of this mass graveyard.

The third general point is that I think you should take time off to force yourself outside your comfort zone, and I use *zone* here mostly as a metaphor for a "mental zone," albeit it can refer to an actual geographic zone as well in case you choose to travel like I did. In fact, forcing yourself outside of your geographic comfort zone can greatly help you in forcing yourself outside of your mental comfort zone. If you are in your typical environment, it can be very challenging to escape your usual thought patterns. When I was in London, I was surrounded by my friends, many of whom worked in financial services; I was frequenting restaurants, bars, and clubs, where I kept on running into those friends and more people from the industry; I almost instinctively picked up the *Financial Times* every weekday; and so on.

Was it then to be a surprise that my thoughts, even once I had stopped working, included how the financial markets were doing, how various hedge funds were performing, which financial firm I could perhaps work at next, even if it was in a new location? Once I was out of London, my personal geographic comfort zone, those thoughts never fully went away, but they were increasingly diluted by new ideas. It was in the teahouses on the foothills of Everest that I first thought about entrepreneurial ideas for Brazil.

Now, this process of leaving your comfort zone does not always have to mean a literal, geographic act of leaving one's city. The fact that I had to travel away from London, one of the most exciting cities in the world, with myriad opportunities from every walk of life, is probably more testament to my own inability to mentally detach myself. Other people might be able to leave their mental comfort zone while physically remaining in their city. Angelina started to take advantage of London a little bit more even before we started traveling, doing things she never had done before, even if it was as simple as taking some yoga classes. In fact, after we stopped traveling, had decided to move to Brazil, and I was making initial arrangements in São Paulo, she spent a couple of months in New York taking a whole range of classes.

It is a sign of how much I was entrenched in my comfort zone that I initially had a plan B: I was interviewing at a New York hedge fund to be the head of the future London office. I went through something like five interview rounds, with the final round taking place just hours before I boarded a plane from New York to Bangkok, where I was to meet Angelina and embark on our first big trip. I remember sitting in the conference room that day, with every portfolio manager and analyst from the hedge fund listening to my analysis of EADS, a European aerospace company, as an investment opportunity. I was mechanically "going through the motions" with my mind, but my heart was in faraway places; I was talking without passion. About two weeks later, one late night in our hotel room in Kathmandu, I got to talk to one of the fund's partners who informed me that they decided not to offer me the job. I made some polite small talk, hung up the phone, and told Angelina, who was busy packing our equipment for the hike up to Everest base camp the next morning. She just said, "I'm happy." This would usually appear to be a very odd thing to say to your partner after he was just turned down for a job, in fact, definite grounds for a relationship fight. However, Angelina meant it with her heart; she knew this was the best outcome for me, and for her too. And it was not only because, had I been accepted, I would have re-entered the hedge fund world one year before the worst financial crisis in living memory, and probably would not have earned any money, and possibly quickly lost my new job. Angelina and I had our concerns about the markets at the time, but we did not foresee the extent of what was to come. The important point was that the final connection to my old comfort zone had been severed; the golden handcuffs were off. We were now truly free to explore a new life.

CHAPTER 4

DECISION AFTERMATH

Deciding to move to São Paulo that morning in front of the Santo Grão coffee shop was the easy part. Yet it was like deciding to get married: the simple decision carried with it an infinite tail of planning. Where would we live? What would we do? How would we legally stay in the country? How would we learn the language? Even mundane stuff crossed our minds, like how to open a bank account. Thankfully, we did not face some of the decisions that many others have to look at (e.g., how would we find a school for the kids?) and the additional tail of follow-on questions *that* includes.

Nevertheless, broadly speaking, the kinds of questions will be the same for anyone undertaking this kind of move. However, the sequence and way in which you have to tackle them will depend on your personal circumstances. Those who move via a transfer with a company obviously already know what their job will be; their company may organize their entire move; their company may also sponsor their work visa; they may have the help of a relocation consultant, who helps to find an apartment, open a bank account, find a gym, and with other things of everyday life; their company may offer language training. Those were the kinds of luxuries I enjoyed in my moves to London, New York, and Tokyo. In Brazil we would have none of this, and, frankly, I was kind of excited about it. I knew that, if I ultimately was to do something entrepreneurial, there would not forever be some consultant holding my hand—the sooner I would start cutting my teeth in the local environment, the better. In general, though, the comforts of an organized move with a company are nothing to scoff at: for many, especially those harboring entrepreneurial ambitions, but not yet defined ones, and/or those not having sufficient "working capital" to simply live in a place for a while, this type of moving on somebody else's dime may be a good solution. By the time you are ready for an entrepreneurial adventure, you will have already resolved most of the above questions with your company's help, and in the meantime you continue saving up for your investment in your start-up. In fact, I know several expats in Brazil who originally transferred with a company but are now merely staying in their jobs as a springboard to explore other options, in the meantime benefiting from the working capital and other resources that their jobs provide. Of course, there are also drawbacks to this route. Exploring other options in any depth may be very difficult if you are working long hours as e.g. a consultant or investment banker. Furthermore, in most places, if you relocate with a company, you will receive a temporary work visa that is sponsored by and tied to that company. Once you leave that company, there is typically a limited amount of time you have to either change your visa status or leave the country. Then, of course, there is the danger of not managing to leave the mental comfort zone of your job.

Our case was of course different. We definitely were not moving with a company. I was going to explore the entrepreneurial option, and Angelina was going to look for a new, local job. We were fortunate to have sufficient savings to be able to just live for a while without having to start to work immediately. So we decided to tackle the above questions in a certain sequence. First, we would find a place to live, in order to have a local base. In parallel, I would start to do research on the entrepreneurial options for myself, and Angelina would start to research job options for herself. With regard to visas, I would take advantage of a special visa program that Brazil offered for investors: incorporate a company in Brazil and invest at least US$50,000, and receive a five-year visa (the minimum investment has since been raised to R$150,000, approximately US$90,000, and the general conditions of the program have been tightened). I thought this program was a very smart initiative by the Brazilian government to encourage foreign investment by small entrepreneurs like me. Angelina, meanwhile, would continue on a tourist visa (with a maximum of 180 days in the country) until she would obtain a long-term work visa. We would sort out things like bank accounts locally, using our new home base. Angelina wanted to spend some time in New York, to see her family, but also to take some random courses, so we decided that I would move one to two months ahead of her. Nevertheless, in the immediate short-term, we would come back to SP together, mostly in order to look at places to live together, but also for Angelina to meet more potential employers and other contacts, and finally for us to attend a big annual Brazil investment conference. With regard to learning Portuguese, Angelina would take some Portuguese lessons in New York, while I would simply take lessons locally in SP. I had kind of given up on trying to learn Portuguese in London: like for every language, the key was practicing it, and while there were many Brazilians in London, most of them wanted to practice their English.

There is not only planning to do with regard to the destination of your move though. You also need to think about what you need to get done before your move in the place where you currently live. When should you leave your job? What will you do with your current house or apartment? What do you have to communicate to tax and/or other government authorities about your move? When can you sensibly pull your kids out of the local school? What do you have to do with your pets? Thankfully, a lot of these questions did not apply to us. One of the only big questions was what we would do, if anything, with my apartment in Covent Garden. The choices were keeping it as a pied-à-terre, renting it out, or selling it. The rational option would have been to sell it. We both thought that the London real estate market had overheated. However, emotionally I was not ready to sell. First, I really liked my home, it was a rather unique four-storey maisonette, with a big roof terrace, in a very central location, minutes from London's Covent Garden, the Royal Opera House, and a lot of other London West End attractions. Second, we figured that, if unexpectedly we would really hate our new life in Brazil, it would be psychologically good to have a home to go back to easily. In the end, I decided to list the apartment both for sale and for rental anyway, as I figured it would not hurt to get in actual data points about sales and rental prices, even if in the end I may not pursue either option. In November, though, I received a good rental offer, from tenants willing to accept a six-month break clause in the lease (i.e., allowing me to give them notice on the apartment after four months, at which point I thought we would have figured out whether Brazil was for us or not). I accepted the offer. It provided us with additional income from the rent, while also giving us sufficient psychological comfort that the London home was still there, if needed. On the government front, I had to fill in one form informing the British tax authorities that I was moving away and giving up my tax residency—nothing too bad!

Then there is one more important to-do before you move: you have to tell your family and friends all about it. Let us divide this into two parts: first, close relatives and friends, and second, everybody else.

The first group, by definition, is made up of people who matter a lot to you. By extension, their opinions will matter to you. For example, if they think you are somewhat nuts for contemplating the move you are about to make, you actually cannot just brush them off; you have to engage and explain yourself. If some of them argue strongly that you are about to take a wrong decision, this may very well impact your own thinking (i.e., you may start having doubts). So you better be prepared. This does not mean defending your opinion at all costs—after all, the others' doubts may be justified. It just means having done your research, and having thought about it. Frankly, you obviously owe that to yourself anyway, independent of any preparations for discussion with family and friends. In our case, the reactions from close family and friends ranged from "Oh cool, can we visit for Carnival?" to some thinking of us as crazy for wanting to move to a "violent and dangerous" place like Brazil. They had obviously heard a smattering of the "shot in the hand" type stories. It was by chance some New Yorkers making the violence point. I personally thought that kind of "cute." I preferred the typically predictable type violence of a robber pointing a gun at you to convince you to take your money and watch to the unpredictable, undifferentiated violence of terrorists attacking a city like New York or London (which I had experienced first-hand in July 2005 in London). I was tempted to, but in the end did not, make that point. We merely pointed out that we would be careful and prudent in our day-to-day life. Maybe we would even buy a bulletproof car like some of our Brazilian friends had (I secretly thought this somewhat cool and James Bondesque). Besides, I had already lived almost four years in an environment where there had always been a danger of being robbed at gunpoint—at university: Penn is located in West Philadelphia, which at least during my college years at times could be a rough neighborhood. I actually did get assaulted at gunpoint during my last year in college (I should point out that, in the meantime, West Philadelphia had improved a lot, in part thanks to the university's community-building initiatives). In any event, ultimately we managed our relatives, promising caution, and dangling the perspective of caipirinha-fueled visits around Carnival time.

As for the second group—everybody else (friends, work contacts, and other acquaintances)—we told some of them personally, but the majority we informed via e-mail. Once again, there were a few replies along the lines of "Great, we'll come for New Year's in Rio," but probably the most notable thing was that, while there was hardly any criticism, there were not really voices cheering us on either. Virtually nobody said, "Right on. Good decision." In fact, even the Brazilians living in London thought we were slightly crazy and/or probably just sick of the London weather and wanting to be on a beach in Rio (quite a few male friends also commented that I was probably just moving for the women, never mind I was in a serious relationship). Many of them kept on bringing up issues like the still high levels of violent crime in the country or endemic corruption in politics. Of course, they were also a self-selected group that had consciously decided to move away from Brazil and I now did not really expect them to argue in favor of their country—unless they were preparing to imminently move themselves, which they were not. Very smart investment professionals, like the portfolio manager of the hedge fund where I had interviewed, refused to touch Brazil, a country that had managed to turn several currencies into confetti during its history. I was actually happy about all of this. It confirmed that, despite more than four years of decent politics and stable macroeconomic performance at that point, Brazil was still largely a contrarian's story at the time. Remember, this was (Northern Hemisphere) autumn 2007 and things were still a lot different both in London and in Brazil. Notwithstanding beginning symptoms of the credit crisis and related financial market jitters, London and New York were still seen as the undisputed business centers of the world, and as aspirational locations of the highest level at least for professional life, and maybe even for life in general. If you could make it there, you could make it anywhere. It was where the most absurd compensation packages were paid and the most lavish parties held. Brazil, on the other hand, like a number of other interesting emerging markets, was generally still regarded at best as a risky up-and-coming place and at worst as permanent backwater with insuperable structural issues. Brazil had not yet been one of the last countries to enter the global financial crisis and one of the first to exit. The country had not yet received investment grade ratings. Rio had not yet won the 2016 Olympics. The *Economist* cover story about "Brazil taking off," with Rio's Christ the Redeemer statue shown as a launching rocket, had not yet been published. Nor had there yet been the *Wallpaper* cover story calling Brazil "the most exciting country on earth," showing supermodel Alessandra Ambrosio on a São Paulo skyscraper roof. Even the large pre-salt offshore deepwater oil fields had not yet been discovered. All of this was yet to come, but at that point, we could generally not expect a whole lot of enthusiastic support from friends and family. We needed to have our own conviction, and that was just the way I liked it. Besides, this type of inertia of established opinions is the perceptive investor's friend: it is exactly what allows you to buy assets at good value, like Brazilian real estate. If everybody had agreed to the Brazil story already, prices would have been a lot higher. Correspondingly, there was inertia of opinions about life and the economic situation in places like London and New York. Like I said, I did not foresee how bad the crisis got in the end (if I had, I would have made the appropriate trades and made a lot more money). However, I am always paranoid about having inertia in my own opinions. I have learned that volatility of everything is one of the only certainties in life, and its extent can often be bigger and its movements more violent that you think. I sometimes played these scenarios through in my mind. Just as São Paulo could go from a Latin American backwater to one of the key economic centers in the world, I knew that at least in theory change to a similar extent, and probably in an inverse direction, could happen in London. Perhaps the overload in debt, already noticeable in those days, could crash the British economy. Consumption would suffer disproportionally, and many of the shops in my street in Covent Garden could close. The area could become quieter. Concurrently, government would probably have to cut spending on everything, including the police forces. Crime would probably pick up, assaults could increase in my neighborhood, graffiti on the streets, more drunk fights of dissatisfied people. Real estate values could plummet. In the end, I did not believe in this scenario. If I had, I would have rushed to sell my house in London, which I did not. However, I also knew that the probability of this scenario was probably much higher than general public opinion at the time believed it to be. Volatility is a reality of life, and it is usually greater than you expect—just another reason to force yourself out of your comfort zone.

In addition to the mass e-mail to everybody, and the personal conversation with close family and friends, there was one more very important element with regard to publicizing our move with those constituencies, one that you must not skip: we had a massive leaving party. We rented out a set of rooms at London's Hempel Hotel, centrally located in Bayswater. We played Brazilian music and also rented a karaoke system. We invited maybe 150 guests, of which between half and two-thirds showed up. Some others sent messages. Some did not show and did not send messages. It was the beginning of the filtering process of friends and acquaintances that happens in every move. In any event, we had a blast. You always have to leave a place on a high note like that.

WHERE WILL WE STAY IN BRAZIL?

Even before the leaving party, we returned to São Paulo to resolve the issue of where we would live, a.k.a. finding the home base. The choices were staying in a hotel, renting, or buying a place. The first option was out; we both loved the Emiliano hotel, but our commitment to Brazil was open-ended enough that we did not want to stay in a smallish hotel room for weeks or possibly months, not to mention pay the daily hotel rate (not even a corporate rate using our former business cards). Renting a place in Brazil, as we found out, is not entirely straightforward, as one needs to get around the problem of giving the landlord some comfort that one will actually pay the rent. This typically involves getting a guarantor (we did not have anybody in Brazil that we felt comfortable to approach to act as one), or getting a type of insurance (virtually unattainable for nonresidents), or, if the landlord was up for it, simply prepaying a lot of the rent. It also did not help that the duration of Brazilian residential rental contracts is often very long (twenty-four to thirty-six months). Just as, at least at that point, we wanted to keep some flexibility on the London end, we also were not keen to commit to a three-year contract in Brazil.

In the end, I decided to buy. This might seem odd given I just talked about flexibility; owning a property may appear a lot more of a commitment than even a three-year rental contract. However, I liked the idea of investing in Brazilian real estate. At the time, it was possible to purchase apartments in prime regions in SP, in a good state and in decent buildings, for around US$2,000 per square meter. That seemed too cheap. Not only did I have a good idea about real estate prices in cities like New York or London or Paris, I also had a notion about prices in other emerging market centers, such as Moscow, Hong Kong, Shanghai, Mumbai, and Dubai. SP was the one city that was "off the chart," in a positive, value-for-money, sense. Statistics confirmed this notion. For example, Global Property Guide, a website listing key cities worldwide by residential square-meter prices, ranked São Paulo somewhere in the 70s, behind cities such as Tallinn in Estonia, Phnom Penh in Cambodia, San Juan in Puerto Rico, and Limassol in Cyprus. Moscow, Singapore, Mumbai, Dubai, and Hong Kong were all in the top fifteen. It is true that the SP metro region as such still has land available, and hence there will be a flow of new supply of buildings. However, new build in traditional, high-end, centrally located neighborhoods was virtually impossible; here, supply was almost as constrained as in the traditional beach neighborhoods of Rio de Janeiro (of which I will speak later on).

Deciding to buy a place in São Paulo in one way was like deciding to move to Brazil: it was a quick decision as such but carried with it a tail of planning and to-dos.

First step was to find a property. A search on Google led us to some listings websites. The majority of listings were by brokers. We were very wary about some unethical broker offloading some overpriced property on us. We really needed somebody we could have minimum trust in.

This of course was a general truth for moving to a new place and building a life and business there: you need people you can trust. I believe in something I call the "chain of trust," which works like this: You start with a handful of people in whom you already trust, perhaps because you have sufficient history with them, or perhaps because they are equally dependent on you for something. From there, you just ask for referrals of people who may help you with what you need. The referring may go down several levels (i.e., one of your original trusted persons refers a contact, who in turn refers a contact, and so on). What matters is that each referral is a solid, trusted one, rather than just some acquaintance that the referrer does not know so well. One litmus test is that you should think that the referrer would feel bad if the referred person ended up giving you bad advice, or worse.

For the house-hunting, we asked some of our London-referred SP contacts to indicate real estate brokers. Who really came through, though, was one of the locals, Roberta, who we had met at the social network dinner in SP. After the mini beach vacation in Cabo, I had returned to SP for a few days and, among other things, had a couple of coffees with Roberta, and we became friends. It turned out that Roberta, as part of the services offered by her relocation company, also found apartments for people. The fact that she was well connected in SP society, and hence often got to know early about high-end properties, helped quite a bit too. And so, before our house-hunting trip, I asked Roberta whether she could preselect some properties for viewing. She managed to preselect more than a dozen.

We had to give her some minimum specs of our dream property first. Location—that was simple—Angelina and I agreed on: within walking distance of the Santo Grão coffee shop. I think if the second floor of Santo Grão had been available, we would have bought or rented it—it felt like a homey refuge in this new city. Then there was the question of space. As I mentioned, square-meter prices were less than a tenth of the prices in good London neighborhoods at the time. This could have worked two ways. One, we could have continued to have a perfectly reasonably sized apartment (in London, we had about 1,500 square feet for the two of us, and this was plenty, I thought). Two, we could, if we wanted, massively upgrade on space. Option two was all too simple to rationalize: "we are going to get married and have kids, hence we need space." Heaven knows why we could not just admit to ourselves that after years of living in places like New York and London, we loved the novelty value of space. In any event, the brief to Roberta was clear: above 3,000 square feet, please.

In September 2007 Angelina and I traveled to SP to look at a lot of apartments, mostly chosen by Roberta.

We focused on apartments rather than houses, even though SP has a number of centrally located residential areas with some fantastic houses, including at times large gardens with swimming pools. This was because we wanted the additional safety factor of having doormen. We had heard our share of stories of break-ins in houses, at times while the residents were in the house, which typically meant hours spent tied up and at gunpoint. The apartments we saw were in buildings that ranged from about forty years old to brand new. New buildings command a considerable price premium, sometimes over 100 percent in comparison with older buildings. I immediately thought of this as an opportunity, as renovation costs in Brazil are still relatively low (the labor cost part, that is; of course you can spend as much as you want on materials). Also, old buildings typically have more generous floor plans, as opposed to not uncommon three-bedrooms-in-1,000 square feet layouts in new buildings. On a lesser note, older buildings typically do not have heliports, and I was not too excited about the idea of sunbathing on the terrace of my apartment while somebody landed a helicopter right above. To be fair, I should point out that there are some rational reasons as to why the gap between old and new building prices exists (even with fully renovated old apartments). New buildings often have generous leisure facilities, such as pools, saunas, gyms, tennis courts, event spaces, etc. For us, this was irrelevant, but many Brazilians, especially with young children, like the leisure facilities. Furthermore, new buildings come with more garage space. For the type of spacious apartments we were looking for, it was not uncommon to get five or more dedicated underground parking spaces in a new building, sometimes up to ten. So why would anyone need ten parking spaces? Well, let us suppose a family with four driving-age members may have six cars, plus perhaps a couple of the house staff may arrive by car too. Then add some spaces for guests (albeit buildings typically have extra guest parking spaces anyway). The number of cars is partly explained by the absence of a comprehensive public transport system (and upper-class Brazilians' typical disdain for using the few public transport options that do exist). SP has also enacted a regulation whereby every car (license plate, to be accurate) is prohibited from being used during rush-hour periods one day per week (this is called *rodizio*). Looking at the clogged thoroughfares of SP defies believing that this regulation actually exists. Anyway, the regulation has also given an additional impulse to car sales, as many richer people simply buy an additional car to use on the day when their main car is restricted, which further explains the need for many parking spaces. We did not plan on having a fleet of cars, hence we did not care about the number of parking spots. Therefore, we quickly directed our search toward the older buildings, with the more attractive prices and better floor plans. Given that focus on older buildings and the type of property we were looking at, we seemed to end up with a disproportional number of landlords of the elder widower or divorcée type, who were invariably curiously eyeing the young expat couple. We saw some apartments with a random broker, too, whom I had contacted. That did not work so well. On a couple of occasions, we were taken to totally different neighborhoods to see totally different types of properties from what we had specified.

In the end, the winner was the first apartment that Roberta had shown us—a 6,000 square foot duplex on the fifteenth and sixteenth floors of a roughly thirty-year old building, about a two-minute walk from Santo Grão, with no leisure facilities whatsoever, and an embarrassingly meager allotment of two parking spots. It was owned by an elderly Uruguayan entrepreneur, who had moved there with his wife and seven children after having been robbed in the house where they had previously lived. By now, he had moved back to Uruguay with his wife, and of his children, only one daughter remained living in the huge apartment, which he probably rightly thought somewhat excessive (I made sure to point out that we were planning to have a family in order to fill the apartment). He was also clearly unmotivated to organize a major move and quickly started talking about selling the apartment with all furniture. That was a godsend. I really did not fancy the thought of shopping for furniture for

6,000 square feet; it probably would have ended up being an apartment with ultraminimalist decor. I sensed bargaining power, too, because it was clear that not wanting to move was a matter of avoiding hassle for the current owner, not a matter of money. "Fifty thousand dollar for everything. What do you think?" he asked, referring to the furniture. "I give you fifteen," I replied. "Fine." "Great trade," I thought.

We quickly settled the issue of the price for the property. I negotiated and managed to get around 10 percent off the asking price. At that point, I felt comfortable that it was good value, partly due to the prices of the other properties we had seen, and also partly due to my additional research on the Internet. I also did not want to risk losing what I thought was a remarkable opportunity by trying to negotiate another 5 percent or so off; after all, I had high conviction that Brazilian property prices had significant upside potential. We agreed a move-in date, mid-December 2007. So the main commercial points were settled between the principals of the transaction; now I *just* had to figure out how to actually legally buy a property in Brazil. Because the property-buying project had gone really well so far (after all, we found a great apartment within one week), I naturally asked Roberta for recommendations. She gave me a choice of three lawyers that she trusted. I chose one of her indications, whose daytime main job actually was to work in a so-called *cartório*. A cartório is basically a government-approved notary-type office that handles virtually every important official document in your life—from marriage certificates to property titles. It is also the place where you register your signature, and afterward the cartório can authenticate its veracity whenever needed. Cartórios are simply an indispensable part of Brazilian bureaucratic life, and therefore also of the property-buying process, and they can have very long lines. Hence I liked the idea of having somebody who moonlighted as a property lawyer but was also a cartório official; surely he could accelerate things if and when needed. The property-buying process in Brazil is actually not that complicated. Once you have negotiated the terms, you typically execute a private sales and purchase agreement and make a down payment, normally 10 percent. At that point, both sides have basically locked in the deal, subject to due diligence. After this follows a period of typically a few weeks to verify all necessary documentation on the property and the seller. If something does not check out (e.g., the property has a massive tax liability), you can walk away from the deal and get your down payment back. If everything is fine, the buyer and seller then execute the official title transfer deed (*escritura* in Portuguese) and the buyer pays the balance of the purchase price. The buyer also has to pay some taxes and fees, typically around 3 percent of the property purchase value (this depends on the municipality) as stated in the deed (which may or may not be the real value). In Brazil, most properties are freehold properties (i.e., you own the land); however, there are some leasehold properties too (i.e., somebody else owns the land, often the federal government), where you have to pay a transfer tax on purchase, typically 5 percent. Perhaps most important, there are few restrictions on foreigners buying properties in Brazil. At that time, in 2007, the only restrictions I knew of were with regard to lands in the Amazon area. However, in mid-2010, the government started requiring majority national ownership for agricultural land. There continue to be no restrictions, though, for you to purchase your dream beachfront apartment in Rio.

For this first purchase, the process went by and large smoothly. There was an initial scare, when my lawyer took quite a while to prepare the first contract draft and the seller called me to say that it was taking too long and that another potential purchaser had appeared. I was willing to change lawyers at a moment's notice, if necessary, but one phone call from me in London to the lawyer in SP resolved the issue (this was the first time I learned the lesson that, in Brazil, one call can resolve what many e-mails cannot). I also reassured the buyer, reminding him that I was going to pay cash, generally move very quickly, and take the furniture off his hands. The documents were all OK. My main concern was about the exchange rate from U.S. dollar to Brazilian real. The Brazilian real was strengthening a lot, and I had actually agreed a U.S. dollar price with the seller (i.e., the sale price in real kept on declining). Virtually every day, before the signature of the purchase and sale agreement, I expected a call from the seller wanting to renegotiate the price, but it never came. By mid-November, everything was settled—the whole process from starting the search to closing had taken about two months. The final oddity was with regard to the actual payments. First, being a nonresident, I had no way of opening a bank account in Brazil. Second, escrow is pretty much unheard of in Brazilian property transactions. So the process of transferring money became somewhat of a trust exercise, but everything went fine.

Now is a good time to remember how the rest of the book is organized, as the actual move to and life in Brazil really starts now. I decided to conceptually divide my experiences into some big buckets, realms of life of sorts. Those buckets are professional life, social life (anything from friends to sports), romantic life (yep, romantic relationships, in any sort of depth and with various degrees of success), and language. I thought about writing the book from here on in chapters organized around these buckets, but in the end I thought that this would end up giving the book too much of an appearance of a mere practical guide. Instead, the book is intended to tell a fun story and hopefully in the process will give out advice, or at least points to think about. So I decided to keep it in the order in which life happens—chronological—but I will touch upon all the buckets.

So here we go.

In this prearrival in Brazil phase, really the most important bucket was the professional one. My romantic life was, for now at least, sorted. Making new friends, other social activities, and learning the language, would wait until I arrived in Brazil, which was scheduled for mid-November 2007.

WHAT SHOULD I DO IN BRAZIL?
In the professional realm, there was one obvious question: what would I do in Brazil? After more than six months of traveling, I actually started to feel a professional void in my life—I needed to work, or at least I needed a project. It had to be a serious project too. At some point while traveling, I had actually thought about working in a dive shop (and ideally moonlighting in a dive *bar* at nights) for a few months on some tropical island, but that romantic-sounding stereotype really did not sound attractive anymore at the time (by the way, it is starting to sound attractive again now, at the time of writing this book). I needed to find a job, so what could I do?

Going to work for somebody else, especially in finance, of course was always an option. However, I was not ready to put the golden handcuffs back on. I was craving an entrepreneurial experience at this point in my life. It seemed like the logical time to do it: I was thirty-five years old, had gained a decent amount of general business experience, had many contacts, had savings to invest, and also did not have to worry about taking risks as I did not have a family or anybody else depending on me. "If not now, when?" I thought to myself. I would advise anybody else who has an ounce of entrepreneurial zeal in him or her to think the same way: if the time is right, you have to go for it, because you never know when the circumstances may be favorable again.

Clearly this was yet another quick decision with a string of follow-on questions...

WHAT TYPE OF BUSINESS?
I started reading a lot of research reports on Brazil, its economy, industries, and companies (taking advantage of the fact that I still had good relationships with my former brokers at the investment banks who published such reports). In addition, I cannot overstate the value of our experience of simply having been in the country and having observed life

there—when we could ask ourselves simple questions like, among others, "What type of product or service that exists elsewhere is missing here?" or "What aspects of life are too complicated here and should be simplified by some product or service?"

Brazil, in its current phase, is actually full of opportunities, in many sectors. Real estate is interesting because of a huge housing deficit. Consumer financial products, including credit and insurance, are very underpenetrated in comparison with other countries. The energy sector has a number of opportunities, ranging from the effects of the huge newly found oil and gas deposits, to projects in alternative energy, such as wind and solar. Agriculture is an obvious sector, given the world's growing population and need for food, and Brazil's massive quantity of arable land. Any product or service attending the demand of the quickly growing middle class is a good bet—whether it is discount air travel, affordable cosmetic surgery, or something as niche as pet grooming.

So how do you filter and choose? I established some simple criteria. I wanted to find an opportunity in which I could at least somewhat leverage existing experience and contacts—starting from zero did not seem that smart. It had to require a reasonable, manageable amount of capital; I did not want to have to spend a long time trying to raise funds, especially in the worsening fund-raising environment at the time. Neither did I want to pursue any opportunity that was in a regulated industry; I did not yet have any government contacts in Brazil and in any event, it seemed unlikely that a foreigner would be able to get his hands on an attractive opportunity in a regulated industry. Besides, regulation also meant that it would take a longer time to get started.

In the end, I decided to investigate the possibility of starting a mortgage broker in Brazil. I am aware of the irony of this in light of the fact that just around the same time, the mortgage markets in the United States and Europe had started to implode. Brazil was different. I knew from research reports that mortgages were underpenetrated here—the value of the entire mortgage stock in Brazil at the time equaled less than 3 percent of the country's GDP. In comparison, in many developed countries, this number is above 50 percent. In other developing nations such as Mexico, Chile, and Turkey, it is at least above 10 percent. I also understood why this number historically had been so low—due to high and volatile interest rates, and imperfect lender protection—and, more important, why everything was now changing: because the macroeconomic environment had improved, interest rates were coming down and were less volatile, and the government had even enacted new laws to better protect lenders against defaulting mortgages. These insights as such made *any* business in the mortgage value chain a potential opportunity. One of the obvious ideas would have been to set up a specialized mortgage lender (i.e., a financial institution). However, this was rather capital intensive (due to minimum equity requirements) and heavily regulated. Mortgage broking, on the other hand, was a low-capital-intensity business, because mortgage brokers are mere intermediaries, without a need to have a balance sheet to lend money. As for the regulations, I honestly had no idea at the time—this was a key question that I had to research. Most important, in mortgage broking, I would not start from zero: while I worked at the hedge fund, we had for a few months been one of the largest shareholders in Germany's largest mortgage broker. I was responsible for that investment and hence got to know the business model of a mortgage broker very well. I also got to know the company's two cofounders (and co-CEOs) quite well.

I was excited that I seemed to have successfully identified an opportunity that ticked the boxes of my criteria. Now I needed to determine its feasibility with certainty, and ultimately write a business plan. Questions included: Would local banks be willing to use and pay mortgage brokers? Would customers understand and like the concept?

Is anybody already doing it? And, like I mentioned, were there any regulations governing this sort of business in Brazil?

I decided to give the Germany mortgage broker a call and try to schedule a meeting with the founders. Successful entrepreneurs that I have met the world over are typically more than willing to lend fledgling entrepreneurs a helping hand. This was no exception: I sent a one-paragraph e-mail outlining my idea for Brazil, and they both quickly agreed to meet. My objectives for that meeting were to confirm my understanding of the business model and to double-check the important questions for my feasibility analysis of the opportunity in Brazil. My medium-term objective would be to see whether the Germans would even be willing to co-invest in a Brazilian venture; with its experience, e.g., with regard to IT and processes in general, I thought that I could accelerate the rollout of the service, avoid many errors, and outpace any potential competitor. In September 2007, I flew to Munich, where the German mortgage broker's headquarters are located, and left the meeting with a clear view of what I had to do to investigate the opportunity. I was more excited than ever. I had had many CEO meetings in my time as an investment banker and as a hedge fund analyst. Yet this time it was not about talking about a deal or investigating an investment in the company. It was about creating something new, something of my own.

The rest of my time before moving, which was not a lot, was spent partly in London and partly on a trip during which I went for an all-around full-day health check in Germany and for one week to a detox spa in Thailand. I guess I wanted to arrive in Brazil with a healthy and cleaned-out body, ready for "retoxing" by the Brazilian party social life. I even managed to squeeze in a few days in Dubai and Teheran (no retoxing in those places, as I traveled during Ramadan, and in any event, alcohol is illegal in Iran).

Just before moving, I read in the news that Jim Rogers, the investor that I so admired, had sold his New York townhouse and was moving his entire family to Singapore. His young daughter was already growing up learning Mandarin from a Chinese nanny. This was all the final endorsement I needed.

THE BRAZILIAN DREAM

São Paulo – as seen from my apartment

CHAPTER 5

BEM-VINDO AO BRASIL

"You're an expatriate. You've lost touch with the soil. You get precious. Fake standards have ruined you. You drink yourself to death. You become obsessed by sex. You spend all your time talking, not working. You are an expatriate, see? You hang around cafés."

—ERNEST HEMINGWAY, THE SUN ALSO RISES

Every move boils down to a moment when you step off an airplane and realize you are there to stay. There is typically no return flight on your ticket. You probably have slightly more luggage on you than when you go on a mere vacation. I had been through that moment already several times in my life. So here I was again, on Monday, November 12, 2007, stepping off a TAM Brazilian Airlines flight from London. I entered the country as a tourist, as I did not have a permanent visa yet. I now had a maximum of

180 days in the country within the next twelve months to sort out my visa situation, and a lot of other things.

Besides not having a permanent visa, I also did not yet have a place to live, so I opted to stay at a hotel until I could move into my newly purchased apartment in mid-December. Wanting to save some money, I decided against simply staying at my favorite "home-away-from-home" Emiliano and instead moved in down the road, in the Regent Park all-suites *apartotel*. The Regent Park is several notches down from the Emiliano in terms of amenities and ambience (e.g., it does not even have a decent gym, so one of my first actions in SP was to sign up on a temporary membership in an external gym), but it was also willing to give me a very good special deal for staying a month there.

I even had a daytime office, a.k.a. the Santo Grão coffee shop, which is fortunately only a few minutes' walk from the Regent Park. I arranged a local cell phone—prepaid, because a postpaid plan required proof of a local address. With basic needs taken care of, there was now no more excuse: I needed to get started on my new life. Needless to say, I had never found myself in such an unstructured environment before. I had to set my own work hours, define my own priorities. There was nobody to report to except for myself.

I decided what to tackle first based on a mixture of necessity and the fact that my Portuguese was awful (I still had to use the English tourist menu at Santo Grão), which effectively precluded me from doing certain things. One of the most urgent things was to get started on the visa process, as I did not really want to either get kicked out of the country after 180 days, or illegally overstay the visa and hope for an amnesty. Because I was hoping to obtain a long-term visa via Brazil's investor visa program, the first step was to incorporate a company in Brazil. There was the additional motivating fact that one cannot receive one's household move until one holds a permanent visa (I now considered myself even more lucky to have bought an apartment including all furniture!). Of course I had no idea about how to incorporate a company in Brazil or even about which types of corporate forms existed, or their relative advantages and disadvantages. I knew I had to outsource, and to somebody who spoke fluent English. I activated the chain of trust and asked some of my SP contacts for referrals to lawyers who could help me. In the end, I contacted four lawyers, sending an e-mail (in English) with a few basic questions about the company formation process in Brazil and a request for each to submit a quote for the full service of setting up the company. The idea was that I would be able to compare notes and end up paying a fee that was competitive. In Brazil, if you need a critical service taken care of, in my experience, it is always best to either hire the most prestigious service provider available, or get at least two others to compare (and maybe even hire both and have them check on each others' work). I chose a young real estate lawyer from a prestigious SP firm, that was also located within walking distance from my home (Regent Park) and office (Santo Grão). She got started right away, in mid-November 2007, on drawing up and filing the necessary documents for a Brazilian Limited company, the chosen corporate form. Limited companies actually need a minimum of two partners in Brazil, with at least one of them being a Brazilian resident. We got around that problem by paying the law firm's accountant a small fee to act as a second partner, with him signing a side agreement that effectively restricted him from making any decisions on the company. Brazilians always find a way to get around things; there is a local expression for it: *jeitinho brasileiro*, meaning "little Brazilian way." While I was at it, I also got the lawyer to double-check the other lawyer's work on the purchase of my apartment, and I asked her to research and write a memo on the important question of regulation of mortgage broking in Brazil. In the meantime I was able to double-check some of the new lawyer's information via the legal department of the German-Brazilian Chamber of Commerce, which was very happy to help a fledgling German entrepreneur in SP.

The other task that I could get started on without speaking decent Portuguese was the business plan, at least parts of it, for my start-up. I could at least define the basic structure and content, and hence implicitly the questions that needed to get answered once I could actually speak enough Portuguese to ask them. I relied on a mix of the pointers that I had received from the German mortgage broker's co-CEOs, a bunch of books and articles on new venture initiation (some from the Internet, some even dating back to my Wharton time), publicly available information on other mortgage brokers (some of them were quoted companies and hence had a lot of information available), and even the business plan for a proposed start-up mortgage broker in Turkey, which a good friend of mine was in the process of seed-funding. Now, even when I started on the above tasks, I knew of course that at some point I would have to fill in some local data points in the business plan, and especially in the financial plan, that could not be answered purely by secondary research on the Internet (and even when I found snippets of some answers on the Internet, I still needed to double-check with somebody). I tried to use my new network in SP as much as possible, especially for more generic questions including, "How much do low-level bank employees earn here?" However, there were some questions for which I needed to ask exactly the right people: "How much commission, if any, would banks be willing to pay to a mortgage broker?" or "How does the mortgage process work in Brazil from the bank's perspective, step-by-step?" I did not have the exact type of people in my network to answer these types of questions, hence I had to find ways to get to them. Cross-referrals, the chain of trust, as always was one way. However, I did not want to rely on merely this solution. One of my additional approaches was to try to find people with exactly the right type of background once more on a social network on the Internet, but this time on LinkedIn, the most prominent professionally oriented rather than purely social network.

I found about half a dozen suitable people and sent e-mails to all of them, in English. Another approach was my standard route to getting information in my hedge fund days: for stock-exchange-listed companies, speak to the investor relations manager. There were a number of publicly listed companies that I had an interest in talking to in order to ask some basic research questions, including all of the big banks and the major real estate developers, as both were potential partners for the new mortgage broker: banks had the products I wanted to sell, and real estate developers had many customers buying apartments who needed mortgages. I managed to schedule a number of company meetings with banks and developers—and luckily most of them spoke good English.

Those were my initial days in SP: during the day, I typically based myself out of Santo Grão, where I got to know the entire menu and entire waitstaff, doing research on the Internet and writing up my business plan, occasionally leaving for a meeting, and caffeinating myself excessively as you would if you based yourself out of a coffee shop.

At night, in those early days, my Brazilian friend Roberta typically picked me up from the hotel at around 09:00 p.m. to go to dinner, and often on to some bar, club, or private party. We were hanging out a lot with the social networks crowd, and there were a lot of classic young expats, on limited-term assignments, who were out to have hard-core fun. One of them, a Belgian consultant, was the archetype. While technically in a long-distance relationship with a serious girlfriend back in Europe, he seemed to hook up with a different Brazilian girl probably every week. It was also he who introduced me to Love Story, also known as LS, an infamous SP nightclub. LS has been around for a long time and is located in the relatively more dangerous (at least at night) historical center of SP. It is an after-hours club that typically gets started at around 04:00 a.m. and goes on until mid-morning, when you emerge from its tacky interior to be virtually blinded by daylight. Its clientele is unlike that of any other SP club—an eclectic mixture including well-to-do locals and expats, gangsters, and prostitutes, some of whom were still working while at LS, some just coming for fun after work. It is not uncommon for people to bring guns to LS. Earlier in 2007 an off-duty police officer took one of the doormen hostage with two guns, after having had a "misunderstanding." More recently, in November 2011, a Love Story client had a fight with the doormen and ended up shooting a couple of police officers in front of the club. The club also has, in my opinion, some of the best music in SP. The first and only time that I went together with the Belgian consultant, we arrived at LS—where everybody greeted him by name—and were immediately ushered to an upstairs VIP area. Minutes later a bottle of vodka appeared, as well as two blondes in ultrashort dresses, who did not look like they were of the "after work" contingent. A mere ten minutes, three songs, and two vodka tonics later, the Belgian came up to me and asked, "What do you think we get some blow, go to the motel next door, and have a foursome?" That right there was a certain type of SP expat experience summarized in one sentence—an experience that was very much there if you wanted it. I declined. If I had wanted to focus on that type of expat life, I probably would have moved to Moscow and partied my brain and liver into oblivion while hunting for red rubies in belly buttons, all the while pretending to work. Yet this is something that I think can perhaps be interesting for maybe six months, or more likely three. I was in SP to try to build something new, exciting, and big. And that required a minimum of discipline, especially with company meetings scheduled early in the morning.

Which is not to say that I did not suffer through a fair number of morning company meetings with a massive hangover, at times slightly nauseous and thinking about the fastest route to the next bathroom in case I needed it.

Thankfully the meetings were still held in English, as I could not have handled Portuguese in that state. However, I knew this was unsustainable – I really had to learn the language. My written Portuguese was actually improving, as I tried to send many e-mails in Portuguese. This is of course much easier than speaking or listening to Portuguese, as I had as much time as I wanted to write an e-mail. Also, when writing e-mails, my main "teacher" was Microsoft Outlook's spell-checker. It would highlight every incorrectly spelled word and hence I could find out the error and avoid it the next time. I also tried learning with books, and it helped me understand basic grammar rules. For vocabulary I used mostly virtual flash cards. I started reading books and highlighted and looked up any word that I did not know. I had not taken any classes yet, as I had not yet received a referral for a good teacher.

 I knew that I urgently had to improve my spoken Portuguese; company meetings in English would not continue forever. Especially when—and I hoped this would be in the near future—I was going to meet, for example, with mid-level staff at banks to talk about my distributing their mortgage products, the probability that those meetings could be in English would drop considerably. I simply had to be able to speak and understand Portuguese, to have comprehensive conversations with fluency. Some people had advised me to watch TV in Portuguese, especially the famous telenovelas, which are like Brazilian versions of American or British soap operas, only tackier…which is why I could not get myself to watch them. However, there were quite a few TV shows that I *did* like, hence I decided to just watch those, even if they all happened to be American TV shows that were dubbed from English into Portuguese. Some series are actually intolerable to watch in their dubbed versions, usually because the voice of one or more of the main characters sounds terrible in the new language, such as Homer's voice in *The Simpsons*. Still, there were lots of other options. I started with *Frasier* and quickly moved to *24*, of which I watched several seasons in Portuguese (always with subtitles switched on).

My research process required me to speed up on my Portuguese learning at that point though. First, I had gained the cultural insight that phone calls were a lot more effective than sending e-mails. I had sent out a considerable number of research e-mails with questions to various organizations, typically to people I had never spoken to before. My reply rate to those e-mails was virtually zero, and I initially figured that people simply did not want to help me out. However, when I eventually managed to call (or, rather, have somebody else call) following up on the e-mail, the majority of people were perfectly willing to help me out; they just had not wanted to respond to the "cold call" e-mail. Furthermore, my secondary research on the Internet yielded some meetings to be set up. I had found some smaller banks, who offered mortgages but did not have extensive branch networks, and could hence be particularly interested in using a mortgage broker as a distribution channel. These were not public banks though (i.e., there was no investor relations department that I could use as an easy entry point). I literally had to call up a switchboard and work my way through possibly a number of people, explaining what I was proposing (which was unheard of in Brazil) until I perhaps got to the right person in the end. That *clearly* was beyond the scope of my current Portuguese.

I enlisted the help of various people. First, I paid a friend of a friend who had offered to give me Portuguese lessons to do these initial calls on my behalf and give me written summaries afterward. Once we found the right conversation partners, and it was time to schedule meetings, the assistant of the business center of my hotel became my key ally—she basically pretended to be my secretary. Last, I had to find a solution to conduct the meetings in case the participants really did not speak any English—which was actually the majority of times. For this, I borrowed an intern of the law firm that was working on incorporating my company, who pretended to be my junior associate. I thought I was starting to become quite good at the *jeitinho brasileiro*.

The meetings actually went quite well. It seemed like I had found at least a couple of banks willing to distribute their products through me and pay a reasonable level of commission. In the meetings I even increasingly tried to chip in comments and questions directly in Portuguese, rather than speaking English and going through my "junior associate" as a translator. It was often funny to watch the reactions of the participants of the meetings to this proposal, by a gringo who had arrived in Brazil only weeks earlier, to set up a brand-new business concept in Brazil. I think it was a mix of incredulity and pity, along the lines of "this poor guy is so nuts, we should help him."

Even my "cold call" e-mails on LinkedIn had triggered one response, from Juan Pablo, an Argentine who had lived in Brazil for decades and had vast experience in consumer finance and was generally well connected. He also had strong entrepreneurial drive, having set up two brand-new businesses within the company where he was a director. Juan met me for a quick lunch, found my idea intriguing, and put me in touch with a number of people, including the CFO of the largest real estate broker in Brazil, and the CEO of a brand-new mortgage lender, BM Sua Casa (the first such institution in Brazil).

In the BM Sua Casa meeting, I got particularly bold, speaking mostly in Portuguese, never mind the fact that I only understood about a third of what was being said in response; I figured I could always ask Juan afterward, as he participated in the meeting. At one point, in the middle of explaining my business concept, the CEO and one of his deputies looked attentively at me from across the meeting table as I had just stopped talking mid-sentence. As several seconds went by, it became clear that

I was not making a pause for intonation or emphasis, but I really had no idea what to say next, and by *next*, in this case, I literally mean the next word. My brain was frantically trying, but failing, to find the Portuguese term for "down payment." Instead of giving me what I was looking for (*entrada*), my brain kept flashing a bunch of words in my mind along the lines of *bomba nuclear* and *terrorista*. Eventually I sighed, politely switched the conversation to English, and made a mental note that learning Portuguese by watching dubbed episodes of *24* was not such a great idea after all.

My Portuguese for social interactions also left lots to be desired. Like in business meetings, I had gotten increasingly bold about simply trying to speak Portuguese with friends (and like in business meetings, I only understood a fraction of what was said in response; the problem is that, once your counterpart thinks you actually have a reasonable command of a language, he or she no longer consciously slows himself or herself down or simplifies the language, but simply switches into native language mode—at which point it was game over for me, at least at the time). One evening, during a conversation about skydiving, I wanted to call the Brazilian girl that I was with a "chicken" (incorrectly assuming that the colloquial American term for coward, "chicken," somehow translates into the same meaning in Portuguese—it does not) and instead inadvertently ended up calling her something like a "slut." After the "bomba nuclear" and "slut" experiences, I got the point that it was time to start formal Portuguese lessons in the new year.

The day of moving into my new apartment finally arrived in mid-December 2007. As I walked through the apartment, I could not believe the quantity of things that were still there, which the previous owner had simply left. I knew that I had agreed to buy a furnished apartment, but what I found was better than a hotel. There were towels, linens, hundreds of books, flat-screen TVs, stereos, DVD players, kitchen equipment and utensils, a fully stocked bar including bottles of imported champagne (astronomically expensive in Brazil), and even a couple of family photo albums (OK, the latter ones the previous owner had forgotten to take along, as it later turned out). This guy really did not want to deal with moving.

I also eventually inherited the previous owner's maid and one other staff member. I had consciously decided to do this, as the previous owner had employed his staff for more than ten years and found them trustworthy. In Brazil, or any other place in the world, this is clearly worth a lot and is better than trying to find people from scratch. The maid asked me (in Portuguese, as she did not speak any English—yet another motivation to speed up my Portuguese studies) what I preferred to eat, and whether I wanted her to buy any specific groceries (fortunately, she did not ask about headache money). I was sitting on my terrace in the sunshine, overlooking SP and just said for now she should buy everything necessary to make caipirinhas, including some passion fruit. Lifestyle-wise, I thought I was starting to live the dream.

Besides unpacking your suitcases and having a caipirinha on your terrace, there is clearly one more thing to do in a new home: have a party. I did not want to do anything massive, though, leaving the real housewarming party for the new year, after Angelina's arrival. So I invited some twenty people, my "usual" new SP posse. It was a civilized affair, having wine and caipirinhas in my living room, while listening to Brazilian music. Nothing crazy happened, nobody wanted to have a foursome. Yet when I spoke on the phone to Angelina before going to sleep, as I did every day, she was mortally pissed off that I had given a "housewarming party" without her. I did not understand the reaction at the time. I knew a couple of things though. One, any situation like a move is an inherently stressful one and hence, if you do move while in a relationship, that relationship will be stress-tested; any issue in the relationship, no matter how deeply it is normally buried, will likely surface. Two, Brazil had its own challenges, particularly for expat women, as I already knew from our experience in Rio.

The other annoyance at the time was that my company's tax registration process, and hence my overall visa process, had stalled. My lawyer explained that the tax authorities were investigating the new company. This was of course ludicrous, as the company was brand new and had no history, but there was nothing we could do. My lawyer told me she could not give me any reliable estimate on timing—we were talking about Brazilian bureaucrats, and it did not help that we were approaching the holiday season. There it was, my first taste of Brazilian bureaucracy.

I left SP for the holidays on December 22. Version 1.0 of the business plan was ready, and I felt very good about that. I also was settled in the new apartment, never mind it was full of somebody else's stuff. Virtually on the last day before I left, my company's tax registration number was finally issued. Portuguese was still an issue, but I knew I would resolve it. All in all, any initial anxiety about the move, if there ever was any, had passed. I genuinely felt comfortable in my new environment, even after only one and a half months.

I passed Christmas in Germany, attended one of my nephew's weddings there, and spent New Year's with Angelina and a group of friends skiing in Meribel in France, where I discovered an additional, unwanted impact of learning Portuguese. When some Frenchman asked me for directions in the street in Meribel, my response automatically came in Portuguese; I was unable to access my previously fluent French, at least in the first moment. Both being Romance languages, I guess they were similar enough to cause this level of confusion. Plus, I did not exactly speak a lot of French in São Paulo. As always with languages, it was "use it or lose it." I was no stranger to this, unfortunately.

My Japanese had already gone from once fluent to being reduced to using sound bites when ordering sushi. I was not too happy about it, but Portuguese would be much more important in my future life than French.

In the 2008 Rio de Janeiro Carnival parade

CHAPTER 6

SETTLING IN

In mid-January 2008, Angelina and I flew from New York to SP together. I assume Angelina must have gone through the same sort of "first arrival" emotions as I had. I was more worried about finding a cab (or several) that would fit the eight suitcases that we had brought along. At least Angelina was going to move into a readily set-up apartment, without the need for a month's stay at the Regent Park, I thought.

To some extent, obviously my life changed, as I went from a quasi-bachelor existence to quasi-married, or at least cohabitating, life. There were more couple-y dinners and significantly fewer clubbing party nights, and certainly not at Love Story. Other parts of my life remained the same, as my days were still spent researching and refining the business plan while sipping iced cappuccinos at Santo Grão. Before heading to New York, I had stopped over in Munich to hand over my business plan to the German mortgage broker and to explain my analysis of the opportunity. They were going to analyze it and get back to me with a decision as to whether they wanted to participate. Clearly, I did not want to rely solely on them, so I contacted a few other potential investors as well, through my network.

Besides my business work, though, there were now more and more other tasks encroaching on my new life, some of them annoyingly mundane like…paying bills. It was now January, and, among others, my maid, the municipal tax authority, the electricity company, the cable company, and a raft of other people were looking for money from me. That brought up a whole new issue: how would I pay them? This was fine for the maid, whom I could pay in cash that I could get out of a cash machine with my UK bank card. However, quite a few bills had to be paid by bank debit, from a theoretical bank account that in practice I did not have, and could not have, as banks only allowed permanent residents to open bank accounts. I was sure a *jeitinho brasileiro* had to exist to resolve this issue. I called up a Brazilian friend who conveniently was working at the private banking arm of a large international bank, which even more conveniently was also my bank in other countries. We set up a meeting immediately. Indeed the perspective of a new private client did its magic, and the bank agreed to help me navigate the process. They referred me to a regular branch, which, while unwilling to open a bank account for me as a natural person, agreed to open a bank account for my new company, which I needed anyway in order to deposit the minimum investment required for the type of investor visa that I would apply for imminently. For the visa process itself, in order to completely outsource any necessary use of jeitinhos brasileiros, I hired a so-called *despachante*. The literal translation of *despachante* is "dispatcher," but really these are professionals who specialize in dealing with any type of Brazilian bureaucracy. There are despachantes for clearing goods through customs, for getting your driver's license quicker, for getting municipal permits you need for you business, etc. I thought this US$1,500 was well spent to diminish the time spent on and increase the certainty of getting my visa. I had no intention of emulating some other expats who chose to simply overstay their tourist visas, not leave the country, and either pay a fine at some point or rely on some future amnesty by the government.

There was another semibureaucratic task, though, for which no despachante existed to my knowledge: joining the local country club. The Paulistano club, one of SP's oldest and most prestigious, was located about a thirty-second walk from my new apartment, which was too good to pass up. Like most of the country clubs, it features a gym, several pools, tennis courts, and almost any other sport imaginable. These clubs are members-only organizations, and the process of joining seems somewhat similar to applying to college, involving recommendations and interviews, among other things. I activated the network to at least try to get some of the required six recommendations. Fortunately, it turned out that the *sindico* (something like a tenant's representative) of my apartment building was also a board member of Paulistano. Soon I had my interview. I was also asked to provide a number of *certidões*. In Brazil, certidões (certificates) exist for everything: they show whether you have a criminal record, whether you paid all your taxes, etc. They are also yet another source of work and income for both cartórios and despachantes—at this point, you already get the idea of Brazilian bureaucracy. As a final step, the application form, including my photo, was displayed for one month in a public area in the club, in order to give other members a chance to object. Fortunately, nobody did; apparently I had not spent sufficient time in the country yet to make enemies.

I had also finally started to take Portuguese lessons, at the local branch of a global language school. I showed up every morning at 08:30 a.m., coffee in hand, for a forty-five-minute lesson. However, the style of the school was one of emphasizing conversation rather than any sort of formal learning of grammar, which is not a style that the methodic

German in me is particularly fond of. After about twenty lessons, I got tired of having chitchat about my German hometown, the American elections, and Brazilian food, and dropped the classes. I went back to studying with books, *Frasier*, some (but less) *24*, and simply learning by talking to people (turns out I did not have to pay US$60 per hour to have conversations with locals).

CARNIVAL

Despite all of these various tasks, though, Angelina and I were really settling into Brazilian January lifestyle and mood. January is high summer in the Southern Hemisphere and is also a naturally slow time for business, due to its placement between the Christmas holidays and that most revered of Brazilian holidays, Carnival. There was no point in forcing things; business life is simply slower at this time in Brazil, similar to some European countries in August—fewer people are reachable, e-mails and phone calls take longer to get answered (if at all). It is a time of the year to go to the beach a lot and enjoy life. Who were we to disagree with this local custom? We started planning our own Carnival trip, to Rio de Janeiro. Simply watching the samba parades was clearly not enough for us though. Every samba school participating in the parade sells a few spots in their group, as a source of additional income for the school. We paid about US$500 each to walk in the parade with Mangueira, one of Rio's most famous samba schools. You obviously do not get to have a prominent position in the school's group, as the school does not want to jeopardize its chances of winning the Carnival contest. Thus, Angelina unfortunately did not get to wear some ultraskimpy bikini and be a samba dancer on top of a float, but rather we both got to wear enormously bulky costumes, with many colors and many feathers. The hardest part was fitting into a bus in the costumes and then waiting out about four sweating hours while it was finally our school's turn, to walk down Rio's Sambódromo, the purpose-built street lined by stadium seating where the parade is held. The feeling of turning into the seven-hundred-meter Sapucaí street, facing bright floodlights, deafening samba beats, and the cheers of ninety thousand spectators cannot be described—it really needs to be experienced. It was another one of those moments of feeling that we were living the dream.

The Rio Carnival, by the way, is only the internationally best-known one of various Carnivals that exist throughout Brazil. The more popular Carnival among young locals actually takes place in the northeastern city of Salvador, capital of Bahia state, heavily influenced in culture by African heritage, and birthplace of the Axé style of music. In Salvador, instead of a samba parade, there are huge modified trucks, called *trios eletricos*, which feature a band playing on top of the truck, and which ever so slowly drive down a parade route over the course of several hours. You can either watch the trios eletricos pass by from one of many roadside *camarotes*, club-like viewing areas with bars and other amenities, or, much more hard-core, pay for the privilege of walking along with the truck, in a cordoned perimeter around the truck. The latter is called a *bloco* and is heavily secured, by dozens of security guards holding the rope that defines the bloco's perimeter. Access is controlled effectively by a T-shirt (*abada*) that you need to buy as your entry ticket, probably because that way control is visually easy for the security guards and also probably because the bloco's participants often get too drunk to manage to hold onto an entry ticket. Depending on the popularity of the band playing, the abada-entry-ticket can cost up to R$1,000, meaning you may be better off only putting the abada on at the last minute when near the bloco, in order not to risk having it literally stolen off your body. Within the bloco, and herein lies Salvador's notoriety, there is an anything-goes atmosphere, at least with regard to kissing. I went to the Salvador Carnival only once, with the same friend with whom I surfed in Florianópolis and ended up buying excessive amounts of silver surfer jewelry. At the time we did not speak any Portuguese (bad idea in Salvador, which is really a more local carnival), and the four days ended up being somewhat of a train wreck. To begin with, my friend confused the names of the most popular blocos, bought the wrong abadas, and instead of kissing a lot of Brazilian girls, we ended up in the main gay bloco. The next day, my friend somehow managed to hook up with a girl from Minas Gerais state and never managed to "move on" from her for the rest of the time (i.e., somewhat misunderstanding the spirit of the Salvador Carnival). He even invited the girl to visit him in London shortly thereafter. He had to end up leaving his work in the middle of the morning one day to pick her personally up at Heathrow, as the immigration authorities did not quite understand her story of visiting some good friend that she had gotten to know at the Carnival in Brazil one week earlier. It is probably superfluous to point out that going to the Salvador Carnival on your own while in any sort of relationship is considered just cause for immediate breakup in Brazil.

Speaking of big Brazilian celebrations, during this chilled and festive phase, I also got to experience my first Brazilian wedding, of a college classmate of mine, in SP. Brazilian weddings are huge affairs, and it is not uncommon to have more than five hundred guests. My friend's wedding had about seven hundred. I asked him how he knew so many people, and he explained that he had invited about fifty, his fiancée about a hundred, and the rest were guests invited by the families. This is typical for Brazil: families and family life are tremendously important. You cannot get married and fail to invite your distant cousin who you have not seen for twenty years and do not even care about. We attended the ceremony in one of SP's principal synagogues and afterward ate, drank, and danced the night away in one of SP's principal buffets (event spaces with catering, for weddings, anniversaries, and other festivities). Of course there were more samba dancers.

I, on the other hand, did not have to think about planning a five-hundred-plus people wedding anytime soon, though, as the psychological stress of the move took its toll on my relationship. It had brought out sides in each of us that we did not like, and we knew we had to acknowledge this and had to figure out whether this was something we could get through as a couple, or whether we had actually discovered "deal breakers" to our relationship. There was no lack of our trying. We had many dinners conversing about our relationship. We had a few sessions of couple's therapy. We even read and talked about *Men Are from Mars, Women Are from Venus*. Yet in the end, the relationship had failed this crucial stress test. I guess it was better that it happened at that point rather than later, say, after marriage, let alone after having kids. This experience leads me to believe that every serious relationship should go through a stress test like this. Without it, there is really no knowing. Just consider that Angelina and I had managed to trek four weeks in the Himalayas together, spending virtually twenty-four hours a day just with each other, and in absence of Internet, phone, and TV. This would have been sufficient to make many couples I know want to kill each other. By the same token, if you are contemplating a move like mine, it means you have to be aware of the possible implications on your relationship. Your boat will be rocked and when it happens, there will likely be no going back, no option of saying, "Let's just move back and continue to be how we were before." You have been warned, and only you know whether you want to take the risk.

Around the same time, I heard back from the Germany mortgage broker. They decided not to get involved. Their reasons were perfectly rational. They still had a growth business in Germany, and Brazil was just too far away for them to be able to spend meaningful time on the project. A few months later, the news broke that they had sold the company to Dutch bank ING for EUR416 million, which, I figured, must have been an additional reason, if not the key one.

So my life was somewhat thrown into limbo in that first half of 2008. Just a few months after the big move, I had not only lost my relationship, but also the uncertainty in my professional life had increased. I never thought about moving back though. I was way too excited about Brazil, its opportunities, and my new lifestyle. I figured my issues were temporary and trusted that things would work out.

Still, I needed to take a step back, think, and then tackle my life again under the new circumstances. Fortunately, I got plenty of opportunity to take that step back and get some healthy distraction. Just about then I hosted the first big party in the new apartment, still cohosted with Angelina and the last night of our relationship. About ninety people crammed on the principal terrace of the apartment, sipping caipirinhas served by the barmen we had hired. We went on until about 03:00 a.m. and at 07:00 a.m., when I was officially single, I found myself at SP's international airport boarding a flight to Miami. It was the first time in my life that I had to use one of those airsickness bags at takeoff, to the thrill of other nearby passengers. I spent a few days in Miami, clubbing, eating, running on the beach, skydiving, and thinking about things. It was a good thing for me to geographically distance myself from Brazil for a few days at that point, as my new home, as much as I loved it, at that very moment represented the stress of a failed relationship and an uncertain business project. Angelina, who had stayed back in Brazil, had a very stressful time too. While still in Miami, I heard that somebody had stolen her laptop from our apartment during the party. This was of course quite a shock, and we would have never expected a thing like this to happen. Despite reviewing hours of security tape, we never found out whether the culprit was one of the service providers to the party or even one of our guests, but either option was sobering.

When I returned, re-energized, from Miami, I managed to slowly remotivate myself. I decided that I would now simply enjoy my private life, without stressing about relationships.

With regard to my business project, I would continue research, now focusing on more detailed operational issues that were necessary to actually implement the business, such as building an IT platform and hiring key staff. Through the chain of trust, I got referrals to a couple of IT companies, developed the specification of the online platform that my business needed, and asked the IT companies to prepare proposals. Juan and I jointly drew up job descriptions for the couple of key people needed initially—one to focus on partnerships with banks, and one to build the sales side of the business—and we published them on the Internet, in appropriate bulletin boards.

There was one other piece of business plan research that I was keen on conducting: focus groups with real Brazilian consumers, in order to understand their thinking about buying real estate, about getting mortgages, and also about the (in Brazil unknown) concept of a mortgage broker. I had my own preconceived notion about what consumers thought, and certainly most of my Brazilian friends did too, but I still wanted to conduct the focus group to know for sure.

I think it is actually one of the advantages that you can have moving to a new country—the fact, that you can, if you so choose, have the humility of admitting that you do not know anything about the country, and you should look at everything with a fresh set of eyes, verifying facts if and when necessary, rather than having preconceived opinions or even prejudices. This can at times even give you an advantage over the natives, who will naturally think that they know their own culture and their country and its people best. For example, most Brazilians I talked to at the time thought that Brazilian real estate was already overvalued—probably because from their local perspective, prices had already increased a lot in comparison with historical levels. I, on the other hand, benefiting from my objective global comparative analyses rather than subjective opinion, thought it to be very, very good value, and I have been right so far.

The focus groups went well. I obtained a raft of information about how consumers think about the real estate acquisition and mortgage process, and, most important, they all liked the idea of a mortgage broker. Several people even volunteered that they were willing to pay for this service—something that I had not thought about; in fact, my business plan was solely built around bank commissions. I followed the focus groups behind a one-way mirror, listening to the conversations on a headset. When I switched off the simultaneous translation, I still had a very hard time understanding things; the discussion was very quick, and there was a fair amount of slang. I still had a way to go in my Portuguese. There were also some lighter moments of cultural insight. When we asked the question as to what extent people get their partner involved in the mortgage decision-making process, one guy actually asked for clarification: "Do you mean my wife or my girlfriend?"

Now being without a wife or girlfriend myself, I made use of my extra time to start meeting more new people again, mostly referrals from other people I had already met. The most astonishing fact was to realize the level to which people were interconnected in SP, and in Brazil at large. As one of friends phrased it, "Brazil is a village," at least when speaking about a certain social class (as another friend put it, "Brazil is not small, but wealth is not widely distributed"). One day I had lunch with a referral from a friend in Washington, coffee with a referral from a contact in New York, and at night went to one of my focus groups. It turned out that the lunch and coffee contacts were good friends, and the sister of the coffee guy worked at the focus group company. This is not an uncommon situation. It has its advantages (e.g., it facilitates the chain of trust) and its disadvantages (e.g., you can get yourself into complicated situations in dating).

As I was now firmly in the dating scene, I was trying to avoid having dates from the same circle of friends. Brazilian women can be *on average* quite jealous, more so, I think, than their European or American counterparts. Stories abound like the one of a friend of mine whose Brazilian girlfriend forced him to tear out any photos with ex-girlfriends from his photo albums, albeit these are obviously extreme examples. On the other hand, again on average, Brazilian women are passionate in all regards and very dedicated to their families.

Because I was still clueless with regard to dating in Brazil at the time, I sought the advice of any local male friend I had. There were some interesting conversations. One autumn evening I was sitting on my apartment's main terrace, having whisky with a Brazilian friend of mine, about ten years younger than I was, from a prominent local family—a playboy, as they are locally known by too. I was in a melancholic post-relationship, in-the-middle-of-wild-dating-type mood, and at some point I remarked, "You know, so what can you do if don't think you can handle having only one woman the rest of your life? The way I see it, there are three options: One, you find yourself a partner who is 'flexible,' with whom you can have the occasional threesome and the like; two, you can have affairs, but that sort of dishonesty is just destructive, and anyway it's impossible because everybody knows what everybody else is doing in SP; or, three, you can go to the *puteiro*, but I'm really not into *that*." *Puteiro* is the Portuguese term for "brothel," of which there are a few in SP (and in Brazil in general), on all sorts of quality and price levels. They are supposedly busiest during weekday lunch hours and virtually deserted during weekends, reflecting the work and family life rhythm of Brazilian men. My Brazilian male friend did not have to think too much to give his view on what I had just said. "Well, option one, the threesome stuff, is great, but there are very few Brazilian women up for it—they're just too jealous. Option two, having an affair—you shouldn't do that. That's disrespecting your wife.

So really option three is the best—go to the puteiro." I was somewhat baffled and speechless, but I figured I had just had some sort of cultural insight. When I eventually got my thoughts together again, I got curious and asked him, "OK, well, so when you go to the puteiro, though, do you at least always have a different girl in order to enjoy the variety, or do you…" He cut me off. "Oh no, I have my girl, I always go to the same one. I bring her presents too." Now I was even more baffled. It was enough male relationship talk to digest and process for that night. I switched the conversation to football, which in Brazil is, of course, always one easy way out.

I was also in the clubbing scene again, which had gotten more expensive, along with everything else, it seemed, in SP. Before, I was used to paying R$100 minimum consumption to go to a club like Disco. Now, the latest club to open, Mynt (a clone of the Miami Mynt) charged R$250. I also still frequented Love Story every once in a while. One time after a LS night, I found myself waking up in an airplane that had just touched down in Buenos Aires, having no idea where I was and how I got there; I must have left LS as usual early morning and gone straight to the airport, judging from the fact that I also did not have any luggage with me and was wearing mostly black, clubbing-type, clothes. And I was still traveling a lot at the time, due to a concentrated number of weddings and bachelor parties, which was convenient, as it helped me to save on the number of days I had left as a legal visitor to Brazil while my permanent visa was not yet approved.

I think in retrospect all the carefree dating, clubbing, and traveling helped me to deal with and ultimately get rid of pent-up moving and post-moving stress, which I had never had time to reflect upon or process during the move or the equally stressful immediate post-move period.

Fortunately, by mid-2008, good news had started coming in again on various fronts. On a macro level, Brazil had received its first investment grade rating from a credit rating agency. While this did not have any significant direct effect on me, it was good for the economy, and what was good for the economy was also good for the future perspectives of my business—and for my new property holding in Brazil. It also further helped the value of the currency, which was good for me considering I had already brought a significant amount of money into the country to buy my apartment.

My Paulistano country club membership also got approved, in spite of my temporary worries after one of my dates had used the club board member's parking spot in my apartment building and I got a phone call during the night asking me to move the car. My visa came through at the end of May and I became an official permanent resident, with all the advantages, such as finally being able to open a "normal" bank account in my name, and disadvantages, such as having become a tax resident in Brazil too. In the end, the entire investor visa process, including the time required to open the company, had taken six months, which is pretty much what the lawyers had told me at the beginning. I had probably spent a total of some US$4,000 in fees for setting up the company and for paying the despachante for the actual visa process. Today, with additional knowledge and contacts, I probably would not pay even half this amount, but at the time it certainly felt like money well spent.

In general, at the time I felt pretty much settled with regard to my day-to-day life and logistics. I was also benefiting big time by basically inheriting the previous apartment owner's life: I adopted everything from his dentist to his travel agent.

Finally I can use the pool at the Paulistano club, an oasis in the middle of São Paulo

Around June I got a funding offer for the business, from the family office of a friend of mine. Honestly speaking, at the time I was astonished: first, that anybody considered funding a business in Brazil for which only a business plan existed—no product, no technology, no customers, no team—and one written by a *gringo* who had spent less than six months in the country and spoke 24-style Portuguese at best; and, second, that anybody chose to make that kind of offer in the market environment at the time (Bear Stearns had already failed and the financial crisis was under way). To be fair, and as one would expect, the funding offer asked me to give up an enormous amount of equity, and I was unwilling to do this. Fortunately, by that time, I had received the proposals from the IT companies to develop the IT platform for the business, and the development cost was significantly lower than I had expected. Simultaneously, I had identified a few potential candidates for the two initial management positions of the company, and their ask in terms of compensation was also on the low end of my expectations. I made a few calculations and decided that I would fund 100 percent of the start-up of the company myself. At the time my analysis was that either, after some six to nine months, I would decide against the feasibility of the company and call it a day, having lost what I judged to be a tolerable amount of my net worth, or the company would look feasible, and at that point would have at least a team and an IT platform and hence attract a much better valuation in fund-raising.

I hired the initial team of two. Fabio, a Brazilian MBA graduate with more than ten years of experience at Citibank, whom Juan Pablo and I had found through our interview process based on the online job posting, became the person responsible for developing bank partnerships. Marcus, a Brazilian with twenty years of sales experience in various consumer financial firms, and a referral of Juan, was responsible for developing the sales side.

Just a couple of weeks before we got started, while I was on a weekend in Buenos Aires, Juan Pablo sent me a press release by a new company. The press release was self-explanatory: this new company, which had just launched its service, was a mortgage broker, and it had a website ready, three partner banks signed up, and claimed to have several sales offices. I had to take a step back and think. I talked to Juan Pablo, and to my friend who made the funding offer, in order to get a third-party reality check. Then I went for a long run in Buenos Aires's Palermo parks. By the end of the run, I had made my decision: I would go ahead with setting up the business. The mortgage sector in Brazil was anything but a mature, no-growth industry, where one had to worry a lot about competition and market shares. On the contrary, it was a nascent, high-growth sector, an opportunity so big that there naturally was space for many companies in the short term, who would then consolidate into still several companies in the medium term. There was no winner-take-all proposition here, and certainly no early-mover-take-all proposition. Flashing forward a couple of years, I now actually wish there was more competition. This is because the main challenge for our fledgling mortgage broker industry in Brazil is that the concept is unknown. Once you explain it to consumers, they typically love the idea, but the problem is that most Brazilians still do not know what a mortgage broker is and what it does. This is a huge consumer education challenge, requiring significant marketing time and expense. I would rather have more competitors to help get this message out, and to share the marketing cost. Although, for sure, I still would like to have the largest share of industry revenues.

Because I was self-funding the business, I was clearly extremely cost conscious. At the initial stage, I refused to spend money on office space, especially while I was occupying a large apartment by myself. I bought a few extra laptops, a multifunctional print-fax-scan machine, multifunctional phones, a bunch of whiteboards, and other standard office materials, and I allocated one of the rooms in my apartment to each myself and my two new employees. It was sort of a comfortable version of the proverbial Californian garage. Probably with Californian start-ups in mind, I also bought a pinball machine (there goes the cost consciousness, you say, but I paid that one out of my personal account and never reimbursed myself even after we got outside funding). In order to portray a more serious business image (without pinball machine) when needed, in discussions with banks, for example, I rented a nearby virtual office for a relatively low monthly fee. The latter basically meant that we had a good-sounding address, meeting room space in a nice office building when we needed it, and an extra phone number, calls to which would be answered in our company's name by a bilingual secretary who would then transfer the call to us. Our initial tasks, which would keep us busy for many months, centered on developing the processes at the heart of the business. Mortgage broking is of course extremely process-driven. You need an IT platform that can do things such as preselect the best mortgage options based on a customer's profile and then aid in the workflow of accompanying the entire mortgage process of the customer until the loan is paid out. We had tried, and failed, to find commercial off-the-shelf solutions from abroad that we could "tropicalize" (i.e., adapt to local needs, including the language). In some ways, this was comforting, as it also meant there would not be any international company that could enter the local market quickly. Hence, we were developing the IT platform from scratch, in many meetings of many hours at my apartment dining table, which also doubled as the meeting room table (I was too stingy to pay for such long meetings at the virtual office, which charged the meeting room per hour). We also had to form partnerships with banks whose mortgage products we could sell. I chose the path of least resistance and once again called my friendly private banker at the large international bank, which was already using mortgage brokers in many other countries. Sure enough, this approach worked, and the bank became our first signed product partner. On the sales side, we had lots of things to do, including developing a recruiting strategy for salespeople, defining compensation including commission levels for the salespeople, and developing a sales force training program. We also had to create a brand name for the company, create a logo and visual identity, and develop a website. The company's legal name is Ichiban, a Japanese word meaning "number one" that I had always liked, but we judged it to be too difficult and too foreign as a brand name. After a couple of brainstorming meetings about the name, we realized that we collectively had no creative ability whatsoever, so I decided to outsource to a branding agency. I got a couple of recommendations for such agencies through the chain of trust. Within two weeks, the agency came up with a short list of brand names. I had some fun with the short lists of the company names and logos, as I was walking around the streets of SP several times bugging strangers to opine on them—the vast majority of people happily went along with it. All of these many tasks we performed at the same time, in the second half of 2008, within our bare bones team of three, plus a low-cost part-time intern that we had hired from one of SP's universities. Like I said, we had to develop most things from scratch, as our type of business simply did not exist in Brazil, albeit we clearly did extensive research on mortgage brokers that existed in other countries.

All of this happened, of course, against the backdrop of the worst financial crisis since the Great Depression. In Brazil, at that point, we felt very little effect. The Brazilian stock market, unsurprisingly, was down sharply like all other global markets, partly because international investors were withdrawing their money to cover losses elsewhere. The Brazilian currency, the real, too, fell sharply, for the same reasons. At some point, I took advantage and loaded up on some real and some shares of Petrobras, the Brazilian state-controlled oil company. Unfortunately, I was well aware, of course, that on the other side of the Atlantic, my net worth was being negatively affected via the London house that I still owned. For, Angelina, too, the crisis did not turn out so badly: as her old employer, Lehman, went bankrupt, she got a job at a local SP hedge fund. From the point of view of building our new company, I actually somewhat liked the crisis. I thought it would buy us time and eliminate many would-be competitors.

My love life was still relatively unstable, or, in other words, remained somewhat wild. I had tried and given up a long-distance relationship with a girl that I cared a lot for in New York City. Now, I never believed a lot in long-distance relationships, partly from personal experience. One key reason is that I think that when you only have a chance to see each other, say, one long weekend once a month, obviously you will put in maximum effort during that weekend, and you will most likely have a wonderful time. Yet obviously this has nothing to do with "real" life of a couple living in the same city, let alone the same apartment. I think one year of the once-a-month long-distance relationship is probably not even equivalent to one month of a same-city relationship. I felt strongly about this to the extent that if I had had a girlfriend in London at the time of the move who was unwilling or unable to come along, I would either not have moved or I would have broken up. But as life goes, I was willing to give it another shot for the girl in New York, also because there was a possibility that she could manage to move down to Brazil within a couple of years. Suffice to say that on the fifth return flight from New York, my patience had worn out.

There was some potential light at the end of the dating tunnel, though, and it was not even in my friend's style of having a steady girl at the local *puteiro*. I had met a Brazilian girl, Nandi (this is her nickname, with her full name being Maria Fernanda; virtually everybody has a nickname in Brazil). Inadvertently, Nandi, too, came to me via a chain-of-trust referral. It all started when the main terrace of my apartment started leaking on my not-too-happy downstairs neighbor, meaning that I had to hire somebody to renew its waterproof lining. So I asked one of my employees at home (who was basically the previous owner's handyman), the janitor of my building, and my private banker, as I knew she had just renovated her SP apartment. This way, I got three building companies to request quotes. In a way, that I learned to be very common, the quotes I received had an enormous variance, with the most expensive proposal literally more than twice the value of the cheapest one, for the exact same work. The best quote came from the building company that worked with the architect that my private banker had referred to me, who was Nandi. Since I had to do work on the terrace anyway, I figured I might as well make some improvements, such as a Jacuzzi and outdoor home theater, and hired Nandi to redesign the terrace. Hence we ended up spending much more time together and at some point started dating.

Besides having a fun time together, our dating also did wonders for my Portuguese, as we almost exclusively spoke in Portuguese. It seems like an obvious comment now, but if you move to a new country and you are single, dating a local can be tremendously helpful in that sense, and of course frankly in many other ways of cultural acclimatization. Vice versa, if you move as a foreign couple, you have to be careful not to end up spending too much time together speaking in your language. This is particularly true if perhaps your jobs also happen to be in environments where your native language is common, like at times in investment banking and consulting. I have gotten to know a few SP expats who fit this category and still cannot speak Portuguese properly, despite having lived in SP at times for several years. Nandi was also the one who pointed out to me that my spoken Portuguese up to that point was awkward because it was, according to her, full of overly formal and archaic expressions more common in formal written language. It then dawned on me that I had spent too much time revising legal contracts and writing business presentations in Portuguese, and not enough time talking socially. Up to that point, essentially I must have sounded like an overly formal Jack Bauer with a law degree and a thick accent. Fortunately, Nandi fixed that, except for the thick German accent.

Nandi and I were not yet in an exclusive relationship when I tested her Brazilian female jealousy. In 2008 I decided to go on something called the Houseship, basically a chartered three-day cruise from SP's main port town of Santos up to Buzios, a well-known seaside resort in Rio de Janeiro state. The difference to a normal cruise was that this was a quasi-nonstop party, with a club-like area set up on the ship's main pool deck, and about a dozen well-known DJs coming along to play at various times. The only allotted time for sleeping rather than partying was between 06:00 a.m. and mid-day. The crowd was almost exclusively Brazilian, but from all over the country, and very well-to-do, which was understandable given the sky-high prices—the cheapest cabin started at about US2,000 for the three days, and the largest suite went for more than US$10k. When we were checking in at the passenger terminal in Santos, I felt the need to text several of my friends to simply let them know that I had never seen so many beautiful women in one place, not even in Florianópolis. The scene bordered on the bizarre, though, with a large concentration of visible plastic surgery, plus the fact that almost everybody seemed to wear dark shades at all times of the night and day. The latter, I later learned, was due to pupil dilation resulting from use of ecstasy. I was on the Houseship with one of my new buddies from SP. Chris, originally from Switzerland, had moved to Brazil more than ten years ago after winning a journey to Brazil in a samba dancing contest in Switzerland, and, after some initial difficulties, found himself successful in the then legal bingo business. That business had unfortunately recently been declared illegal, pushing Chris's livelihood into a criminal underground that he was not willing to join, but he was still living off the money from the good years. His own duplex penthouse was just a few blocks away from mine, and he organized many wild grill parties on his terrace, which featured a swimming pool that Chris's party guests always seemed to try to have fun in. Chris's apartment featured a game room with about half a dozen pinball machines (he had been national pinball champion a couple of times). We drove to and from the Houseship in his bulletproof BMW. On one hand, Chris sure knew how to live a good life and have fun. On the other hand, he was also a self-made successful entrepreneur in Brazil. And, most important for me, he was very loyal and trustworthy, and helped me a lot with many things in my initial acclimatization period—and I am not only talking about hooking me up with girls during his parties. The girls were of course not an unimportant part of Chris's help, though, and I specifically mean Chris's help in my understanding certain aspects of Brazilian women, like their emotional volatility. I remember one time, when we had yet another barbecue on Chris's terrace, playing Wii and drinking champagne. I had grabbed a new champagne bottle and sprayed a girl, whom I had only first kissed ten minutes earlier, until she was dripping wet. She exploded, released a barrage of Portuguese swearwords at me (most of which I could not even understand yet), and fumingly started to dry herself off and said she would leave. "Shit, I guess I just blew my night," I said to Chris. He just shrugged his shoulders. "Relax. In ten minutes she'll kiss you on the mouth again." Chris was right; it was just normal emotional volatility for a Brazilian girl.

My mortgage business kept taking shape during the second half of 2008. A beta version of our website went live by the end of the year. We had signed bank partnerships with HSBC and also with BM Sua Casa, the new specialized Brazilian mortgage lender, with whose CEO I had the 24 Portuguese blank moment. My sales director had identified an initial group of potential salespeople, mostly contacts of his from his days working for an auto loan company. We figured that would be a good group to start with, given they already had sales experience as well as experience with credit products. Furthermore, auto loans had seen their highest growth days, meaning that a lot of auto loan salespeople were looking for new things to sell. We decided to start by only using indirect salespeople, in other words, non-employed representatives. That way, we only had to pay commissions rather than a fixed salary, as we really did not want the fixed cost at that point. Furthermore, having employees in Brazil is rather expensive, as nonsalary labor costs are extremely high, for things like unemployment insurance, mandatory pension, and daily meal and transportation allowances; these costs can easily add up to something like 70 to 100 percent of the pure salary. Having non-employed representatives hence has the advantage of lower costs, but there was also a key disadvantage: there is always the risk that the representative or the Brazilian authorities (if they find out) can sue the company if they think that the representative is really doing the job of an employee and the company only uses the representative structure to save costs. Worse, Brazilian labor courts are known to find in favor of the employees in the majority of cases. Even worse, with regard to the potential liability arising out of the lawsuit, partners of the company are in practice often not protected by the fact that the company is a "limited" company, as this limited nature effectively does not apply to liabilities arising out of labor or tax issues. There is only one known structure to have representatives that provides decent protection against possible litigation: structuring the relationship between company and representative as that of a franchisor with franchisees. This is hence what we ended up doing, which of course involved a raft of work, such as drafting a comprehensive franchising contract, and something called a franchise offer document.

We developed a training program for these sales representatives, containing modules on mortgages, on our processes and future IT system, and sales techniques. Between me and my two initial employees, we wrote a training manual of almost two hundred pages. In order to convey all that knowledge, we invited the salespeople to an off-site at a three-star-type tacky highway-side conference resort with a fishing pond and Swiss-chalet-type rooms. The most memorable experience for me was my invention of a drinking game with cachaça (Brazilian sugar cane brandy), based on questions on mortgages from the training program. If you could not answer, you had to drink—which admittedly did not really increase the likelihood of answering any further questions correctly, but it was a good method of breaking the ice within the team. We also got ready to hire more internal employees, albeit this did not happen until early 2009. We could not manage without an accountant anymore, either, and I found a decent one through a referral by our lawyer. The key element missing was the IT system, which, while having been fully specified, was still in the programming phase, and it would eventually take until mid-2009 for it to be finished, tested, and ready to go in a very initial version.

With the benefit of hindsight, I should say that, maybe inevitably, we committed many errors in those early days. Our website was too complicated and we have since replaced it with an easier, cleaner one. The brand consultant we hired was too expensive; I now have learned of much cheaper, Internet/crowd-based ways of getting creative work done. Not trusting our own ability to build, manage, and grow what would eventually be a large sales organization ourselves, we hired a consulting firm, which was also relatively expensive and added little value in the end. Our filtering of the salespeople was insufficient, and the training program was too theoretical rather than giving practical day-to-day guidance—of the dozen or so salespeople we trained, there are only two left today. Our focus on the end consumer mortgage customer was too ambitious given the fact that the mortgage broker service really was not known at all in Brazil. We know all of this now, but I guess this type of learning process is part of many, if not the majority of, entrepreneurial stories.

By mid-December 2008, I was ready for a detox vacation again from all the working hard and playing hard during the year, and I returned for a one-week detox at my spa in Koh Samui in Thailand. Reflecting on the year, what stood out was really how steep the learning curve had been, in all aspects of life. For work specifically, I must say that I felt like I learned about ten times as much being an entrepreneur than being a hedge fund analyst (and while working in the hedge fund, I felt like I was learning ten times as much as in investment banking). On any given day, any given hour, I could be CEO, CFO, COO, CTO, head of HR, and so on. I loved the new entrepreneurial role, and I did not want to trade it away again, not even for a year-end bonus, although I did miss that part of my previous life.

There was one final decision to be made in 2008: who to spend New Year's (called *Réveillon* in Brazil) with. This was a big deal, as Réveillon is an important date in Brazil, and spending it with somebody clearly elevated that person to a different level, and raised expectations. I decided to spend it with Nandi on Boipeba, an island in Bahia state of Brazil. On Réveillon night, we "formalized" our relationship, and I was officially in my first relationship with a Brazilian woman.

CHAPTER 7

SETTLING DOWN

We came back to "slow January" once again, and getting anything done was much harder than during the rest of the year. I made sure, anyway, that the IT company kept on working nonstop on the programming of our IT platform. That year Nandi and I decided to escape the Brazilian Carnival and head to Buenos Aires. Despite all my love for Brazilian music and party spirit, I find it difficult to spend Carnival in Brazil every year. It is somewhat like having a heavy classic French meal: it is delicious every once in a while, but you cannot do it all the time. Buenos Aires, for all the reasons I already mentioned earlier, is a classic weekend getaway option from SP—at a mere three-and-a-half-hours' flight time and with lots of flights every day. With SP getting more and more expensive, Buenos Aires's good value also became more and more attractive, especially those US$30 dinners including a bottle of Malbec. We were not the only Brazilians (by now I counted myself as Brazilian) to have figured that out—I heard Portuguese all around me.

Of course this time period, the beginning of 2009, was also just about when the economic crisis seemed at its most severe and global stock markets hit their lows. One day, I got an e-mail from an old colleague with the news that the hedge fund where I previously worked was shutting down. Needless to say, this was far from uncommon in those days. I was still regularly talking to a number of my friends in London and New York and it appeared as if by then more than half of them were out of work. Most of them seemed to have turned at that point into "ex-bankers who lunch" (i.e., doing nothing really, as it seemed pointless to try to look for a new job at that point, at least in finance in those cities). Funnily enough, I gave an interview to the *Washington Post* around that time, which I understood to be about the future projects of people who used to work in finance. It turned out to be a cover page article headlined "Out-of-work Financiers Reap Dividends of Seeing the World" and featured mostly personalities who used to work in finance but were now traveling the world, from Carnival in Brazil to climbing Mount Everest. There were actually only two people in the article, including me, who were working on something. I found it, to put it mildly, a bit insensitive to write an article that detailed the often high-end travel of ex-bankers at the worst time of the crisis, and, probably predictably, the *Washington Post* site was soon filled with banker-bashing reader comments.

Brazil famously was the "last country into the crisis, first one out." However, of course, we felt its effects as well, and not only in the weak stock market and currency. The mortgage market growth had weakened and even showed one month of negative growth. Since the market was so huge, and our opportunity long-term focused, that did not really matter too much to us. The most immediate impact probably was that a number of firms that we had talked to did not exist anymore. Besides our partner, BM Sua Casa, there had been at least two other specialized mortgage lender start-ups, and both of them folded during the crisis, due to the loss of their funding sources. At least one mortgage securitization company that we talked to also put its operations on ice. Closer to home, we received no more news about our initial competitor in Brazil and soon found out that it had gone bust.

I still continued to believe that all of this was an opportunity for us and bought us time, so we carried on business as usual. In late March 2009, version 1.0 of our IT platform was finally ready, albeit of course correcting quirks would take a few more months, and improvements continue until today. The consultants, too, finally delivered a useful output: guidebooks detailing all of our processes, including how to use the new IT platform in the workflow. These were great training and reference materials; we just needed to develop the discipline to keep them updated. With the skeleton of the business being ready—core team, initial salespeople, initial banking partners, IT platform, processes—it was high time to upgrade our structure. We needed a real office, outside of my apartment's former bedrooms, and basic things including a phone system and a data network.

I combined the need for an office with my desire to invest in more local real estate, especially at this time of crisis. I ended up buying a real turn-around bet: the historical center (Centro) of SP. São Paulo is a city like Tokyo or LA that nowadays has various business and residential districts, without a dominant center. Over time, dictated by space, traffic access, and other needs, businesses have kept on moving to new areas. The historic center was, as the name implies, the first business area and remains the location for at least various law firms, as many of the courts are located here. The grand Paulista Avenue became Brazil's Wall Street, with most large banks headquartered along here originally. When filled to capacity, it later lost this title to the Avenida Brigadeiro Faria Lima, where newer, more modern office space was available. Faria Lima, too, became filled to capacity but remains probably the city's most prestigious business address, and therefore commands very high prices for buying and renting. The next business areas to be developed moved farther south along the Pinheiros River. Vila Olímpia and Avenida Berrini did not even exist as business centers until the mid-1970s—in fact, there were many areas considered dangerous no-go zones here, due to the presence of favelas, which today no longer exist. Despite all of this evolution, the historical center, Centro, still has its advantages, among them the best public transport links in the city, good communications network access, and decent building substance, besides the fact that it is quite simply more centrally located between the city's other neighborhoods than some of the newer business districts. The price differential between Centro and other districts was significant, though: in the Centro I could buy for as low as R$100 per square foot at the time, in comparison with typically above R$500 and sometimes much more, in the other business districts. To be fair, there were some clear reasons for this difference. The Centro had been run down and there were a lot of homeless people; it was not an area where you wanted to walk around at night—except to go to Love Story, of course, which is a very good reason, but in that case you arrive by taxi or car at its front door. The buildings in Centro are naturally much older, and many do not even have in-house parking. Nevertheless, I judged the price difference to be too excessive. I also felt that things would now move in the next few years, as the city's trend to develop business districts farther and farther away does not seem sustainable. Furthermore, it was my belief that the municipal government would start to clean up the Centro ahead of the football World Cup in 2014, as it is here that various architectural gems of the city are located, like the Teatro Municipal, a grand European-style theater, and Oscar Niemeyer's famous Copan building, among others.

 In order to find a suitable property, I literally went from building to building talking to doormen. This method is somewhat time-intensive, but it is typically far more preferable to using real estate brokers when trying to find a good deal. Fortunately by now my Portuguese was good enough to do this. I eventually came across an entire floor, technically comprising three separate office suites with three separate titles, in an old Centro office building located in a pedestrian zone (i.e., without parking). The floor was owned by an old ethnic German jeweler who had operated a jewelry workshop on the floor for almost forty years. Indeed, half the floor was an office, but the other half was literally a factory-style environment, with huge machines for melting metals, cutting gemstones, and the like. It was the only such operation that had a (grandfathered) permit in what was otherwise an office building. Most potential buyers surely would have been scared off by this scene, but I had my personal architect, Nandi, who could give me a quick opinion on what it would take to transform this minor industrial zone into a clean modern office environment—which was not a lot (of money nor time). So I bought the whole floor and Nandi oversaw its immediate renovation. I rented out two of the three office suites, using a broker, but, more important, also paying commission to the doormen. The third office suite we used for the mortgage company, by now called FinanciarCasa.

After the renovation, we faced a number of other "new office" tasks, such as getting insurance and the municipal permits to operate an office. In order to deal with this and other administrative stuff, I knew it was time to hire a general assistant. I found an easy option once more: I inherited the assistant of the previous owner of the floor. Because he had worked with her for years and found her trustworthy, this was a great chain-of-trust find, and she still continues as my personal assistant today.

I actually "inherited" the property's previous owner too. This was because he claimed he still needed some office space, and also because he simply was nostalgic about the office/factory. So we struck a deal: for an interim period, he could stay in one of the corner offices, paying a symbolic rent, and we were allowed to use all the rest, including all the furniture he already had. That worked reasonably well, save for the fact that it was obvious that the previous owner really did not have that much more to do during his "workdays." He typically came in around 10:00 a.m., read the paper, prayed, chatted with everybody, and left around 04:00 p.m. When he was not reading, praying, or chatting, though, many times he would simply fall asleep in his office, and we started having quite a few meetings when we could hear loud snoring coming from the corner office, which was slightly distractive, to say the least (let alone hard to explain to business partners). I knew we had to find another office solution soon.

The other major event for FinanciarCasa in the first half of 2009 was its first funding round. This all started with yet another referral, this time a really unexpected one. I still regularly talked to my real estate broker in London, dealing with the rental of my apartment in Covent Garden and monitoring the market for selling too. In one of those conversations, he remarked, "You know, there is actually another person just like you, who owns property in Covent Garden, worked in finance in London, but moved to SP recently to become an entrepreneur." That summary was enough to stir my interest, and in any event I had learned the lesson in life never to dismiss getting to know a potentially interesting person, as you never know what might come from it. I met the new contact, Benjamin, over coffee, and his story was indeed very similar to mine. He, too, had worked first in an investment bank, then in a hedge fund, and then decided to move to Brazil and start a company; in his case he is one of the founders of a company that invests in energy projects. As a side note, Benjamin and I were really only two examples of a group of recently arrived expat-entrepreneurs in SP. Among others, there were also two Americans who started the local arm of real estate brokerage Century 21, and two Dutchmen who were getting ready to start an online insurance broker. Benjamin found FinanciarCasa's business concept highly interesting and shared our vision of the market. I mentioned to him that I was thinking about fund-raising. This was true. I had been self-funding the business up until now and was actually prepared to continue to do so, as I believed in my concept and thought it unnecessary to give up a lot of equity. However, I also figured that having outside investors, even with a small stake, would be a useful element of the process of growing up as a company. It would introduce outside accountability—we would have to provide regular reporting on the performance of the business. I also felt that in the medium term the fact of having outside investors would help me at times with managing my staff. I knew that in family-owned businesses, at times the relationship between employees and owner could grow too cozy, your employees could mistake their boss for their friend, with all that implies. By having outside investors (and a board), I would always have the option of invoking the investors and the board, particularly for unpopular decisions.

I have to admit that in spite of all these deliberations, I had not tried very hard to raise funds. I figured I could always fall back on my network of contacts. I had also started to speak to a Brazilian venture capital firm. However, due to the crisis, these were difficult times for fund-raising. I had actually received an updated investment offer at the beginning of the year from the same family office that had made me the original offer, this time on much improved terms (as they should have been, given that now the company had more structure). The family office, though, got cold feet after a few more bank bankruptcies in Europe and pulled its offer. The Brazilian VC, on the other hand, was taking its time, and I had indeed already been warned that decision time frames could be long, easily a year. So if somebody came long wanting to take a small part of the equity and was willing to move quickly, I was up for it. This is what Benjamin could offer. He, along with four other angels, were willing to invest, subject to a reasonable amount and quick period of due diligence. This initial shareholder group ultimately invested about R$700k in exchange for a roughly 16 percent equity stake, valuing the company at roughly R$3.4 million (at the time, approximately US$1.8 million), which I thought fair for a prerevenue business in the middle of the financial crisis. I could not help remembering at some point the comment that the president of a long-gone-bust Internet incubator made to me when I was an investment banker in early 2000, just before the Internet bubble blew up spectacularly: "The rule of thumb for valuation of a business with just a good business plan is US$10 million." Good-old bubble times…

Speaking of investing, I was busily doubling up my exposure to Brazil at the time of the crisis. I sold a number of investments I still held in Europe and brought the money to Brazil. I also finally—too late, clearly—sold my London house, although admittedly still for a decent price (in another serendipity, the buyer of my house turned out to be the partner of a UK private equity professional who happened to be the key shareholder in the UK's largest mortgage broker; so, in another totally unexpected referral, I was later in the year able to meet the founder and chairman of that mortgage broker on a visit to London). I took a trip with Nandi to London to sign the sales contract of the house and stayed in it one final time for a few days. I was worried I might get nostalgic and possibly even change my mind. However, I did not feel that way. While I loved my London house, I had no problem letting go. I even remember that after the first day in the house for a while, at some point I thought to myself, "Gee, this place is so small." Clearly I had gotten used to my new space in SP. I was not sure whether that was necessarily a good thing.

So what did I do with all this new capital in Brazil? The stock markets still scared me somewhat, and in any event I still thought Brazilian property was a no-brainer opportunity, so I continued real estate shopping, walking the streets every once in a while to find opportunities. I soon found a huge, old apartment in the high-end residential neighborhood of Higienópolis. The previous owners had combined two apartments into one very big one. I knew that liquidity was much better for the original smaller size, so once more I went through the renovation numbers with Nandi and ended up hiring her to split the apartment into two again and give them a very sleek updated look. By the way, this type of buy-renovate-sell or buy-renovate-rent real estate investment model—so common, for example, in London a few years ago—is not yet done by many people in SP, and therefore there are real opportunities to make a good deal. Walking the streets one Saturday, I found a very well-located house for commercial use in the up-and-coming neighborhood of Pinheiros. I liked Pinheiros because it was wedged between the fashionable neighborhoods of Jardins (where my original apartment is located), Itaim (home to the Faria Lima business street), and Alto de Pinheiros (a leafy residential area), yet Pinheiros commanded much lower square-meter prices than the other three neighborhoods. I thought this would all start to change, as a brand-new subway line was being built straight through Pinheiros, which would attract more businesses. I also liked the idea of using a house like this one as the office of FinanciarCasa. We would be able to use its streetfront to set up a concept store on the ground floor, where we could serve clients, and that we could show to potential franchisees as well as to our banking partners. In the rest of the house, we would set up our headquarter offices. I managed to negotiate a good price, and Nandi started yet another renovation, turning the house into FinanciarCasa's new main office. That concluded my real estate buying spree for 2009. I had actually looked at buying an apartment in Rio as well, but in the end I decided I had spent enough money already. That turned out to be a very stupid decision.

FinanciarCasa's sales representatives had meanwhile started working in their cities. We received our first check with customer revenue in April 2009—R$1,200. Unfortunately, due to the crisis, the mortgage areas in many banks were somewhat in limbo, including in our partner banks. The partner bank that handled our first client's mortgage restructured its mortgage department just about then, in April 2009. As a result, the mortgage process of that client got delayed to an admittedly unreasonable extent, and a couple of months later, we ended up refunding the fee that the customer had paid us. In general, sales volumes were rather low, running at less than one mortgage per salesperson per month, when the medium-term target was to get to at least five. From what I could tell, many of the franchisees were not very proactive in their selling, which I did not get, because this was supposedly their livelihood. Juan Pablo had already warned me that finding good, driven, motivated people would be the key challenge. I also heard the same complaint speaking to another expat entrepreneur who was also running a franchise-based sales operation.

We were not making more than a few thousand reais in revenue each month. This did not immediately kill us, as we had funding and we kept our costs very low. But of course it really raised a question mark about feasibility and attractiveness of the business. I sure as hell did not want to waste my time in a business that did not have the potential to become a multimillion-dollar profit business within a reasonable time frame, say five years. First, my opportunity cost was just too high (i.e., the money I could earn working in finance again). Second, there were enough entrepreneurial opportunities in Brazil, so it really did not make sense to stick to a mediocre one. So around June/July 2009, I hit a motivational low, and I had many doubts about the business and myself. This is something that entrepreneurial author Seth Godin calls "the dip" and has written an entire book about—that dip in your business when you have to decide whether it is just a temporary thing and you have to get through it, or whether it means that you were actually wrong and should abandon the business and do something else. I did not quit. I still believed in every argument that I had originally made for the business. If anything, these arguments were stronger.

Brazil's economy was doing even better than expected, including the real estate sector. There were more and more banks offering mortgage products, thereby increasing the value of an independent mortgage broker. The opportunity was there and valid. Perhaps our timing was slightly too early. However, mostly, I figured, we *just* needed to improve our execution.

I started a number of initiatives. If franchisees did not work so well, it meant that either we were recruiting the wrong ones, or our training was not ideal, or it was simply the wrong model and we should use direct, employed salespeople. The plain truth was that our business model was so new and untested in Brazil that we simply did not know what would work best; to some extent, we had to try everything. I decided that we should, during the rest of the year, develop an in-house sales capacity, by hiring at least one in-house salesperson. In order to get clients for these salespeople, we would use Google AdWords and a PR agency that would try to place articles on mortgages, mentioning FinanciarCasa, in the media. We thought these to be cost-effective routes of advertising, which would critically also allow us to explain our concept to the target audience (those clicking on a Google ad would end up on our website, where there was a lot of information). Our business concept was brand new in Brazil, still unknown, and therefore needed explanation—a simple ad in a newspaper just did not do the job. We even, through a referral from one of our angel investors, got an entire advertising class at a prestigious local marketing university to think about marketing campaigns for FinanciarCasa, as a class project. This yielded a few ideas, including a YouTube marketing video that we still use today. In order to help with all of these new tasks, I was lucky enough to have been able to hire a summer intern from my old university, the Wharton School. Gerardo was a Mexican who, like me, strongly believed in Brazil and was keen to get on-the-ground experience in some form. Funnily enough, he also wrote, with others, a fictitious account of FinanciarCasa for the Wharton magazine, in which the business was not going so well during the crisis and I ended up giving up buying a motorcycle because of cash crunch concerns. Fortunately this did not turn out to be a prophetic article.

The most significant new initiative for FinanciarCasa, though, was a slight shift, an addition really, to our business plan. This was something that I cannot take credit for myself, as it came out in discussions with our banking partners, but at least I think we were alert enough to perceive the opportunity and seize it. The additional service that we would start to offer was taking care of the mortgage processes of the customers of real estate developers. A lot of residential real estate sales in Brazil are currently sales of brand-new apartments by real estate developers. Historically, before there were a lot of bank mortgages around, the developers actually financed their customers, offering payment plans over several years. Nowadays, with quite a few banks around offering mortgages, most developers rightly see this financing activity as noncore. They still finance apartment buyers during the construction phase (the real estate market in Brazil is so hot that many buildings get sold out preconstruction), as banks cannot offer mortgages as long as a building is not ready and there are no individualized title documents yet. However, once the building is (almost) ready, the developers basically want their invested capital back as quickly as possible (i.e., they either want the customer to pay up with his own cash or via a mortgage with a bank—and they want this process to happen as quickly as possible).

FinanciarCasa's service as a mortgage broker of course has two main parts: one, we can select the best mortgage product options for the customer; two, we accompany the whole process, until the loan gets paid out, always trying to accelerate it when possible. The first part, selecting a bank/product, very often all but falls away when working with large developers, as the bank that financed the construction of the building is typically trying very hard to get the end buyers too (e.g., by offering a special interest rate and other favorable conditions). However, the second part, accompanying the entire process and making sure it completes quickly, still applies. Hence large developers hire FinanciarCasa (and other companies like us) to take care of the mortgage processes of the end buyers of the units in their buildings. For us, this is a good opportunity. We get to use the same systems and processes that we already developed for our "retail" arm. The revenue per mortgage in the work with developers is often lower than in the retail work, but the volumes are obviously much higher.

On the retail side, we have to find clients one by one. In the work with developers (what I started calling the "wholesale" business), a typical building can have something like two hundred apartments, and sometimes much more. We were lucky enough, by pure coincidence, that one of our better franchisees had identified a wholesale opportunity, with a smaller SP-based developer, working on a residential building with about forty units. For us, this was a convenient test run to learn more about the process of working with developers, before we would go on to do much bigger projects with well-known developers, where there would be very little tolerance for errors. I was excited again. Here was a good-looking opportunity to build a decent-sized business quickly after all. Sure, we nudged the business plan, but I had read enough books on entrepreneurship to know that this was completely normal in the life of a new company. I decided that FinanciarCasa would from then on have two businesses: retail (traditional mortgage brokerage for individual end customers) and wholesale (the work with the developers). I gave each division to one of my original two employees.

By then, it was almost time to move into our new offices, the renovated house in Pinheiros. Only there was one more thing to do: have a party. This was particularly true as the house I had bought came with a garage, a small annex building, and a small, paved courtyard garden with a huge pitangueira (a Brazilian fruit tree) in the middle. The FinanciarCasa offices and concept store would only take up the space in the main house—the other spaces had no discernable use for the business. The garden was so charming, though, that I felt it needed to be used to host a party. One evening in August 2009, about 150 people crammed in the garden, annex room, and garage, listening to live jazz until around three in the morning. Everybody had a great time. Then the following day it dawned on me: why not have regular parties in this space…or, even better, open up a bar?

The idea of opening a bar was something I found very attractive. I had always loved giving parties and generally hosting people, and having a bar would just be an institutionalized version of this. I had already thought about trying a gastronomic venture for a little while. Gastronomy was also generally a better business proposition in SP than in many other parts of the world, especially cities such as London or New York, as margins in SP are inherently better. This is because food and drink prices in SP are on par with prices of major first-world cities, but labor costs remain relatively low. I had been invited to consider co-investments in a couple of restaurants in SP already, but both were larger investments with many partners involved. The latter is not an uncommon characteristic in gastronomic ventures in SP; in fact, I know several restaurants and clubs that have more than half a dozen partners. Predictably, such businesses many times suffer from internal management disputes and fall apart after a short while. I had no desire for this and was looking for an opportunity that required a smaller investment, that hence would present limited risk and that I could do either myself or with maybe one other partner. I particularly liked the idea of a lounge bar, a comfortable, cozy space, where guests can have good drinks, some quality snacks, and listen to cool music, played at a volume that easily permits conversations. There was a distinct lack of this sort of space in SP at the time. The city boasts an amazing restaurant scene, with tons of restaurants of all cuisines and price levels. SP's food scene really benefits from the city's melting-pot character and the food cultures that those historical immigrants brought from, among other countries, Portugal, Spain, Italy, Lebanon, and Japan. In SP, you can have authentic sushi, real Lebanese kibbeh, and high-end French food whenever you want. The D.O.M. restaurant in Jardins, around the corner from my apartment, was voted one of the world's top ten by *Restaurant* magazine, and in my opinion there are at least two other restaurants in the city on the same level. For late-night entertainment, SP has a raft of dance clubs, ranging from the chic to the hardcore. Only the segment between, bars, was in dire need of more choice. There were a few bars already, of course, but way too few for a city of SP's size and class. I was intent on helping to fill this void.

The first step was to check with the municipal authorities whether it would be possible to get a permit for a bar in this location. I, of course, hired a despachante to do this, and the quick feedback was positive. There were no restrictions at all—we even could have live music and be open as long as we want. One of my girlfriend Nandi's best friends, Fernanda, joined me as an equal partner in the bar venture. She had some secondhand gastronomy experience as she had already invested in her sister's restaurant in SP and brasserie in Paris, and, more important, she is a person I trust. We then drew up a timetable and tasks to be completed. The most time-critical were design and renovation of the space, which we outsourced to Nandi. Getting the municipal permits we gave to the despachante. Fernanda and I divvied up other tasks such as drawing up a food and drinks menu, contacting suppliers, and interviewing potential staff. This side project kept us busy throughout the rest of 2009.

Even though there were no lounge bars that I liked in SP (yet) and I was in a steady relationship, I would still occasionally go out, of course. I was much more focused on dinners, though, and also started to attend events of another couple of networks I had discovered, like InterNations, an international online-based network of expats that holds monthly gatherings in many expat-rich cities in the world. These types of events were useful in rebalancing my universe of contacts again toward expats, as due to my relationship with Nandi I was spending most of my time with Brazilians. I did not go clubbing that much anymore. By that time, it had also continued to get more expensive in SP, now probably exceeding price levels of London or New York. The most prominent club to open in 2009 in SP was the Pink Elephant, licensing the name from the namesake club in New York, and financed once again by a big group of partners. I actually knew one of the partners and hence fortunately did not have to pay the cover charge, but I could not help notice that at least on certain nights the male minimum consumption was R$350. Tables started at around R$3,000. At the bar, there was not even the usual domestic Brazilian sparkling wine (Chandon, R$50 a bottle in the supermarket, and typically R$80–R$120 in restaurants) available—only imported French champagne, starting at R$75 per glass. Pink also smartly understood how to make its newly rich, very young crowd spend more. Putting fireworks on champagne bottles, so that everybody could see the bottle arriving at your table, was already par for the course in SP. Pink took the ostentatious game to a new level though: if you ordered a certain minimum size and type of magnum bottle, or a minimum number of normal-size champagne bottles, the DJ would stop whatever he was playing and play the *Superman* theme. Needless to say there were still lots of fireworks. Not infrequently after such an order, another table, not wanting to stay behind, also made an order worthy of *Superman* and fireworks. Pink's one-night record for such orders was apparently eight times. I did not care much for this type of ostentation. In fact, Fernanda and I agreed that it was not something that we wanted in our bar. Therefore, we did not use fireworks, certainly no theme songs, and we also put an unofficial minimum age of twenty-five. However, I am aware that this is simply not an uncommon type of behavior in emerging markets, where wealth for many is a novelty. I remembered the orange Aston Martins in Beijing. For entrepreneurs who know how to play to the desires of the new upper class in these places, there are plenty of business opportunities to part the newly rich from some of their money.

Pink was not the only visible symbol of new wealth in SP; there were already many others. A new flagship real estate development, Cidade Jardim, opened, where penthouses cost in excess of R$30 million and the attached mall houses shops of virtually every luxury brand, including a branch of local darling clothing store Daslu. A new Ferrari and Maserati showroom opened, too, and there certainly was an ever-increasing number of such cars on the streets of SP. I should point out that due to protective tariffs, imported cars (or rather any imported goods) are very expensive in Brazil. A Ferrari can cost about R$1.7 million, or, at current exchange rates, around US$1 million. Even so, you can sometimes sip your cappuccino on Santo Grão's terrace on a Sunday morning and see half a dozen Ferraris drive by, slowly, but making sure to howl their engines at some point. Given the lack of weekend destinations reachable by quality roads, driving your Ferrari down the one kilometer or so of the fashionable Oscar Freire street may be the main use of the car in São Paulo. Often the drivers seem to be young kids of the professional playboy-heir type, who probably had been at Pink Elephant just hours before until they got sick of the *Superman* theme. Given the price tag, driving a Ferrari in SP is also a wholly different sort of statement about your social position than in London, where post-crisis one could buy used Ferraris for about GBP30k, and even before the crisis the cars were within financial reach of mid-level investment bankers. By the way, importing used cars to Brazil is illegal, so there was not even any arbitrage available in terms of buying the used cars in Europe and shipping them to Brazil.

I did not have, and still do not have, my own car in SP. This makes me a bit of a freak in the minds of some Brazilians. A girlfriend of Nandi's once remarked that she would not date a man without a car. In my own dating, I had met at least a couple of girls who, while still willing to date me, would show up in their cars but then hand me the keys and ask me to drive. I really was not keen on driving in SP. The European in me likes walking everywhere, and fortunately my home and office are close enough together to do this. When I have to go to meetings during the day, I take taxis, which are allowed to use bus lanes on the big streets, thereby avoiding some of the increasingly horrendous traffic caused by a rising middle class buying more and more cars to fill their many apartment parking spots. At night, I take taxis anyway, even without traffic, as I refuse to drink and drive, which—and I really hate to say this—does not seem to be an attitude shared by all locals (fortunately the police is nowadays running quite a few roadblocks at night, called "Blitz", checking for drunk drivers). Taxis are not cheap but still economically beat cars hands down unless you drive a lot. Just parking your own car at restaurants is expensive, as the standard parking option is valet parking and costs between R$15-25. There was one justifiable use for a car, though: going on weekend trips. From SP, there are a few nice weekend destinations reachable by car. They include all of the beaches on SP state's northern coast (Litoral Norte), the stunning island of Ilhabela (via short ride on a car ferry), and the Swiss-style winter mountain resort of Campos de Jordão. The desire to do more weekend trips, occasional larger shopping runs, and to placate certain types of girls does occasionally make me consider getting a car, typically about once every six months. Yet I would only ever buy a nice car, which by definition means imported, which means ridiculously expensive, which means I, being used to European and American car prices, can psychologically not get myself to do it. So I am constantly trying to come up with schemes to get around the high car prices.

My scheme for 2009 was based on the fact that I heard that diplomats were not subject to the import tariffs. I figured I should investigate becoming the SP honorary consul for some small country, calculating that any sort of investment I would have to make could easily be less than the money I would save on the car. Unfortunately, halfway into my research I was told that the tariff exemption does not apply to honorary consuls. I postponed further scheming and the car buying to 2010.

Fortunately I did not have to worry too much about Pink or cars, as I was in a steady relationship with Nandi, who also conveniently had her own car (and she did not even force me to drive it). Partying nights got replaced by dinners, Saturday family lunches, and parties at friends' houses. It was frankly good to leave the party scene a bit and enjoy this Brazilian quasi-family life. In general, I socialized a lot with new Brazilian friends and got to vicariously live through a lot of ups and downs in their lives, and mostly through a lot of relationship dramas. I heard my share of stories involving jealousy, suspected cheating, and sometimes proven cheating. In a typical story, a woman got regularly cheated on by her husband, but it was always the woman on the other side who received most of the blame and was called a slut, even if she happened to be single. Now that is a level of machismo that my European mind simply could not yet comprehend (later on I would get an explanation). Around the same time, I had dinner with a European friend, married to a Brazilian, chatting about Brazilian love life. He showed me an e-mail on his Blackberry that he had recently received from a Brazilian male friend of his. His friend basically was summarizing, for several other friends, how he had gotten laid six times with six different girls over the past two weeks, including detailing how each of the six girls was either married or at least in a relationship. As he took back his Blackberry, my friend remarked something along the lines of, "Gee, I hope my Brazilian wife does not do that," paused for a pensive moment, and added, "But wait a second, that's what each of the other six guys think!" This type of anecdote at least made me begin to understand the occasionally high level of jealousy that I had seen—sometimes there was a legitimate reason.

One of the events with friends that stood out in 2009 was a wedding. This was not only because the wedding was a stylish affair and the couple is great, but it was also because Brazil's President Lula was part of the wedding party, and so was my girlfriend, Nandi, as she had introduced the couple. It was a Brazilian affair in terms of size, with hundreds of guests, held at a country estate about two hours outside of SP. After the ceremony, Lula and his wife, Dona Marisa, participated in the dinner, but we knew they would not stay to party the entire night but take off for Brasília with the nearby presidential helicopter at a certain hour. There were at least a dozen black-clad Brazilian equivalents of the Secret Service scattered around the party, but Lula was entirely accessible. I guess if you are the most popular politician on earth you do not have to worry as much as some other global political figures.

I told Nandi we should go speak to Lula. She was hesitant, saying she thought it was a bit tacky and even inappropriate—she didn't have anything to talk about with the president. "You know, you will feel much worse afterward for not having gone to speak to him than you will feel if you do," I said. She thought for a moment and relented. The bridal couple was standing next to the president, and when the groom saw us, he pulled us close, introduced us, and mentioned how Nandi had introduced the couple and was therefore responsible for the wedding. As we were motioned into position to take a picture, I whispered into Lula's ear "Look, I'm German, I used to live in London, but I came to Brazil almost two years ago, and I invested in a new business here, because I believe that Brazil is the country of the future. I believe in the reforms that are happening." I figured that was a better entry line than telling him that Brazil's tax code and labor laws were anti small business and stifling entrepreneurship—I shall leave that for any encounter with the next president. Lula turned away from the camera toward me, grabbed me with both arms, shaking me slightly and said, "And you can believe that, you can." Then we went into a five-minute conversation on the various reforms and the optimism for Brazil's future. Lula easily rattled off a set of social statistics comparing Brazil's improvements to other developing countries; he knew his numbers cold. He was also very excited about the recent large oil discoveries and how the proceeds from the oil would be used to further develop the society. At some point the groom interrupted and said, "You know, Mr. President, he is investing a lot, and he is hiring new employees all the time." That was music in the ears of the veteran trade unionist; at that point he just hugged and kissed me. He finished by saying that he would soon go to Germany on a state visit. I told him to say "hi to Angela [Merkel]." It was a quick five minutes, but the president's charisma was impressive, as one would expect. More important, so was the passion for Brazil that I could see in his eyes.

A few weeks later, President Lula was in Copenhagen for the award ceremony for the host city of the 2016 Summer Olympics. The four finalists were Chicago, Madrid, Rio de Janeiro, and Tokyo. My personal bet was on Madrid, but I had really hoped Rio would win. And so it did, of course, with Lula famously crying in the press conference afterward. I was thrilled. Rio, Brazil, Latin America indeed, deserved to host the Olympics for the first time. Rio had done a great job of hosting the 2007 Pan American Games, as I had witnessed firsthand. I also felt like a complete jerk for not having bought an apartment in Rio yet; surely now prices would spike up. Shortly thereafter, the *Economist* published its cover story "Brazil taking off" and during the remaining two months of the year, at least a couple of friends that I remember, both working in finance in London, contacted me to talk about the possibility of moving to and working in Brazil. The Brazil story had started to become more mainstream.

Of course despite all the excitement, there were still a lot of issues in the country, and occasional reminders of them. I had so far fortunately escaped any direct experience with crime in Brazil. However, one weekday, around noon in plain daylight on a street in my neighborhood Jardins, arguably the best neigborhood in SP, a couple of scruffy-looking kids ran up from behind me and yanked my iPhone out of my hand that I had carelessly carried out in the open. I tried to run after them for a short while, but they had disappeared. On a much more serious note, a police helicopter got shot down in a favela drug war in Rio just a few weeks after the Olympics announcement. Resolving the societal issues of Brazil is an evolutionary process; it will not happen overnight, but I believe we are on the right track. There is also no point in remaining a permanent pessimist.

I am an optimist by nature, and by the end of 2009, I felt very optimistic indeed. Everything in my life felt more settled down. I was in a comfortable routine between sleeping in my or Nandi's apartment, working out at the Paulistano club, and spending my workdays at FinanciarCasa's new office in Pinheiros—albeit I still often left the office and went to work at the Santo Grão coffee shop for a few hours at least once a week. Even my bills were getting paid off a bank account in my proper name. In another example of routine that I could do without, I got to file my first Brazilian tax return, and another required document, a statement of all my overseas assets, along with it. Brazil is actually one of the few countries that taxes you on worldwide income. American citizens are used to this, but for the rest of us, it is an awful concept.

The business, FinanciarCasa, also appeared to plod along fine with its new strategy of focusing on real estate developers and individual customers. Particularly, the wholesale business with real estate developers continued to be very promising. We had received one project each to work on from two of the largest and best-known real estate developers in Brazil, Cyrela and Gafisa. The development we handled for Gafisa was located in the Northern Brazilian city of Belém, near the mouth of the Amazon and more than three hours away from SP. We successfully found, trained, and activated a local franchisee there in record time, something that made us optimistic about our ability to expand to other cities. To support these new projects, we had to hire additional staff, and we were now up to five people in total. On the other hand, we had hired several inappropriate franchisees who did not work out at all, despite the time we invested in training. If the whole franchisee model was not flawed, our recruiting method certainly had to be. I put a stop to franchisee recruiting (save for special situations such as Belém) and redirected the retail division's focus to internally generated sales. At least volumes were increasing toward the end of the year, due to internal sales via one of our new employees. On another positive note, we had managed to sign more bank partnership agreements, including with Citibank, Itaú (one of Brazil's largest banks), and Caixa Econômica Federal (CEF), a state-owned bank that had approximately 65 percent market share of mortgage lending. Sometimes, we still got stuck in Brazilian corporate bureaucracy though: one of the large banks claimed it could not sign us up distribution partners because internal guidelines only allowed it to sign up registered real estate brokers; our argument that "customer is customer" did not further our case. Our public relations work also started to pay off, and I started giving interviews to newspapers and magazines. We benefited from the fact that we were a company with an innovative concept in a sector that was considered red hot (real estate).

Those interviews I easily gave in Portuguese, with which I felt very comfortable by then. The only situations in which I still had trouble understanding were those laden with heavy slang, such as in the 2009 Brazilian hit film *Tropa de Elite* (*Elite*

Squad), which is, by the way, well worth seeing in order to understand the interaction of drug traffickers and police in Brazil. At that point, I actually got more concerned about keeping up a high level in proficiency in my other languages, English and German, and I tried to ensure this by regularly reading literature in both.

In a nutshell, by the end of 2009, I was settled down in Brazil, all basic structures of life had been set, and all domains—work, romance, and otherwise—appeared stable. There were no more excuses to be made about my being new to the country; it was time to perform and push on with my projects. I started feeling impatient.

That year, Nandi and I spent New Year's in Punta del Este, a Uruguayan seaside resort that is sometimes called the St. Tropez of Latin America. At two hours' flight time from SP, it is indeed a place well worth visiting, with fantastic restaurants and nightlife, albeit, due to its very southern location, its beaches only get used between December and February. The typical Punta timetable seems to be sleep until mid-day, perhaps go running or otherwise working out if you like, then optionally meet up with friends for a barbecue, or head straight to the beach club, where you will have lunch and drink cleriquot (white wine sangria) for many hours before heading to dinner and then two or three parties or nightclubs, or even one of the casinos, afterward.

Before getting to Punta, I spent a few days over Christmas in Germany as usual, and I even got to make a stopover in Johannesburg to visit a friend. It was the first time I had been to Jo'burg, and it was just about six months before the start of the football World Cup in South Africa. I was impressed by the brand-new infrastructure, an efficient airport, and even an airport train, something we could so far only fantasize about in SP, hoping that Brazil's 2014 football World Cup might bring the same amenities. With my friend, who works in private equity in Sub-Saharan Africa, I spent a lot of time discussing the booming South African economy, and the many investment opportunities throughout several African countries, such as Nigeria, Angola, and Botswana. I loved Brazil, but it was a good reminder that there are still a lot of other exciting places out there.

Copacabana Beach in Rio – where I would finally find an apartment

CHAPTER 8

GETTING SERIOUS

I returned from Punta del Este motivated to get down to business. This time I neither allowed myself to go for my regular one-week detox nor did I allow the Brazilian January to slow me down too much. I just spent one long weekend in Rio, where I used part of the time to update myself on the real estate supply and price levels post the Olympic decision. I did my research via my favorite method of walking the streets I was interested in—in this case Avenida Atlântica, the beachfront street of Copacabana beach—and chatting with the doormen. I actually tried calling about half a dozen realtors, too, whose names I had found listed with specific, interesting-looking properties in the Rio Sunday paper. I had given each broker a crystal-clear brief of what I was looking for and made it equally crystal clear that I was a motivated cash buyer who could move quickly. Nonetheless, out of the half dozen, four never called me back, not even a customer relationship call saying that they may not have anything suitable right now but were still looking. The other two tried to pitch properties that were outside of my criteria but magically always around, or slightly above, the top end of the price range that the brokers had forced me to indicate (as I know this happens, I do not like to give out maximum prices; I usually just say if it's good value, price does not matter; and in any event, I always indicate my desired size in square feet, which implies a price range). I did not find any suitable property on that trip, but I was still very keen on buying in Rio.

At FinanciarCasa, I was keen to grow the business with real estate developers a lot further in order to accelerate growth and get the company to a meaningful size quickly. It seemed that we had so far been doing a good job on our two projects with Cyrela and Gafisa. The developer community in Brazil is, like many specialized business communities, a small one, and we soon benefited from useful referrals and managed to pick up more projects. We hired additional staff accordingly, at this point always preferring to err on the side of hiring too much. We had heard through our industry contacts that most of the few companies offering our type of wholesale service to the developers already had a bad reputation, mostly because they took on projects that were too big and then did not have the internal resources and infrastructure to deliver a quality service. I told my staff that we had to grow, but "in a responsible way," never running the risk of compromising on quality. I actually turned down a few projects that were offered to us at times when I thought they would stretch our resources too thinly.

My favorite side project, SP's new lounge bar, was experiencing its own issues. It was originally supposed to open just after Carnival 2010 (in late February). We had managed to cross off quite a few items on the to-do list. We had received the key municipal permits (at least we thought so). My partner, Fernanda, had somehow unearthed a SP-based French chef who developed a menu for us. I had spoken to pretty much every major liquor company, plus a number of high-end boutique breweries, in order to guarantee the stock for our drinks list. I loved that part, especially the freebies. Soon my office was filled with anything ranging from brewery-branded beer mugs to illuminated Bacardi bat signs, not to mention the free product samples that I made sure to request in every meeting. The renovation of the bar space, meanwhile, had ground to a halt. This was due to a glass roof that we had put over the former garden, enclosing the fruit tree, in order to gain more permanent space. This was a very charming idea in theory, but in practice the roof, with its structure of metal beams and plexiglass panels, was leaking like crazy. We could have had a wet T-shirt contest every time it rained, and in SP it actually rains a lot (almost every day at some point, during the summer). The contractor we had hired for the roof came, and came again, but he just did not seem capable of fixing the problem. I knew this was our fault. We had been too stingy and contracted a cheaper general ironsmith rather than a specialized company with proven experience in constructing such roof structures. It was an example of something for which there is even an idiom in Brazilian Portuguese that translates into: "cheap, but comes out expensive in the end." It's expensive because the remedies you need to take to cure all the problems of the cheap option end up costing more than the original expensive option. Of course the ironsmith had assured us he knew what he was doing. This was unfortunately also not uncommon; at times people tell you they can do a job, in order to get it, even if they do not have a clue. It goes back to a point I already made: in Brazil, many times you are better off just hiring the best and most expensive service provider.

    Meanwhile, Fernanda and I were crash-course-learning everything about the gastronomy business. Even though it was ultimately our plan to hire a manager for the bar, given that we both had day jobs in our companies, we did not want to be clueless. So we learned everything ranging from the sanitary regulations for our kitchen, to what equipment we needed, to how we should find and pay our waitstaff. We primarily got this information from friends of ours who worked in the restaurant business. We still ended up making stupid mistakes (e.g., we bought a ventilation hood for the kitchen that was way too small and had to end up swapping it). The other task that proved more difficult than imagined—I am inclined to say *as always*—was finding a name for the bar. I had hoped that it would be easier than finding a name for the mortgage company, as this time at least there were creative people involved. We scheduled a brainstorming session, with plenty of booze to further aid the creative process. Very late at night, the best suggestions forthcoming were Raphael's Bar and Bar of the Tree. We had to put an end to it. We decided to call the bar JA367 in reference to its street address, Joaquim Antunes 367.

For Carnival, Nandi and I escaped the big party once more, albeit not outside of Brazil. We spent the long weekend at a friend's house on the Ilhabela island some three hours outside of SP, where one can kayak, snorkel, fish, scuba dive, and see the occasional dolphin or even whale.

Coming back, I soon found the retail business of FinanciarCasa in trouble. Two salespeople had decided to quit, leaving behind only the sales director and a very junior support person. We really had to get to the bottom of the flaws in our recruiting process. The salesperson who had left managed to sell a few mortgages in her short time in the company, so it was a shame she left and I made sure to talk to her. She blamed my sales director for flaws in management. I actually thought that was slightly unprofessional, but I also could not ignore a message that I had both been suspecting for a while and had unfortunately already heard from other colleagues. To top things off, I had heard, through our banking partners, that by now newer and less capitalized competitors were selling as much, or even more, than we were. The writing was on the wall. I had to take that decision that I dreaded, but that I knew would come at some point: I had to let go a person who was truly nice, loyal, dedicated, and—based on the record of this previous employment—also competent, but at FinanciarCasa this person did not perform for whatever reason. My guess is that the environment was too unstructured, too "start-up." In the end, the conversation was easier than I thought, as my sales director had seen it coming too. I remembered reading that a typical start-up changes its core management team up to three times until things work.

I learned another lesson in the first half of 2010: in an exciting growth market such as Brazil, you can get tempted by too many opportunities. I did. For me, this happened for a number of reasons in confluence. I had now gained some comfort that the FinanciarCasa business had found a viable model. Furthermore, I still had some money to invest. Last but not least, there was simply the fear of regret of missing a good investment opportunity. It was probably also some type of hangover from my hedge fund days; as a hedge fund analyst I always had about half a dozen investment positions, never just a single one to focus all my time on. Whatever the reasons, I investigated quite a few businesses, in various degrees of depth. My optimistic stance on Brazilian real estate had made me consider starting a Brazilian property fund geared toward international high-net-worth individuals who lacked decent access vehicles to the Brazilian property market. I analyzed this opportunity quite a bit; in fact, I found two partners, we did market research, wrote presentations, researched structures, and even hired lawyers to start implementing the structure. At that point, I decided that the likely absolute returns were too unattractive for the likely time investment, so I pulled the plug, much to the chagrin of my two partners, who continued for another few months but eventually came to the same conclusion. I also looked, with partners, at starting a real estate broker in Rio focused on foreign buyers, for which there is a dire need, as was obvious from my own experience with Rio brokers. For foreigners not speaking

Portuguese (few of the brokers do) and not already versed in the Brazilian property-buying process, the experience is even more intimidating. A third idea, again with partners, was a type of residential building management website, but once more I judged the returns on time to be insufficient. The bottom-line lesson is this: in a market such as Brazil, you can get dazzled by the number of opportunities, but you have to focus and pick the opportunity that you think will give you the highest probability-adjusted financial returns on your time. There is a reason we have the expression "serial entrepreneur," but, at least to my knowledge, do not talk about "parallel entrepreneurs"—a good start-up will take up all your time. As a side observation, many of my would-be partners in these potential ventures were expats and many of them still working at other companies. From this limited sample, it looked like there was a universe of entrepreneurially minded people out there.

I did find a good use for some of my excess liquidity after all: eventually I found an apartment in Rio and, incredibly, through a broker. I had stayed on the ground in Rio for a few days and gave very direct instructions to the broker and very clear feedback whenever we went to see something that was outside my specs. The apartment I found was located, as I wanted, on the Avenida Atlântica, the famous beachfront double carriageway avenue hugging Copacabana's crescent beach.

I was bullish on Copacabana. Famous worldwide and previously Rio's most glamorous beach, Copacabana had lost its glamour to the neighboring beach of Ipanema over the past decades. Copacabana fell into relative decay, while fashionable hotels and restaurants installed themselves in Ipanema and Leblon. Real estate prices in Copacabana were probably on average half, sometimes less, the level of prices in Ipanema and Leblon, and had been for a while. As always, cheap was not enough for investing—there had to be evidence that things were changing. I saw plenty of that evidence in Copacabana. Most important, Help, a famous brothel-nightclub, had recently been shut down, dramatically reducing prostitution in the area. A landmark architectural project, the new Museum of Image and Sound is set to be built on the beachfront strip in 2012, which will class up the surroundings. The city also installed brand-new restaurant and bathroom facilities all along the beach. Private investors had filed plans for several new luxury hotels along the beach, addressing the city's dire need for additional hotel capacity. Nearby favelas had recently been pacified by the installment of permanent police stations inside the favelas. For the 2016 Summer Olympic Games, Copacabana will be one of the event centers, hosting the beach volleyball, triathlon, and marathon swimming competitions. So here was a location that was a globally known brand name, at a huge price discount to neighboring areas. With all of this change going on, I could not resist, especially since I managed to buy at a price approximately 20 percent below the area average.

Perhaps needless to say, I also adore the Rio lifestyle, which for me goes something like this: You wake up to the sunrise over the ocean. Before anything else, it is workout time, perhaps a run along the beach, perhaps Rollerblading, perhaps surfing. Then you hit one of the many juice bars for a healthy breakfast. Perhaps you stop by the supermarket. All of the above so far you can easily do in your bathing suit, if you want, given Rio's relaxed atmosphere. After work, perhaps you take another stroll along the beach, maybe even having a caipirinha at one of the beach kiosks, before heading off to one of the city's many good restaurants.

While I was thinking about all the investment opportunities, the desire for even more liquidity to invest led me to consider doing something that I had contemplated for a while: rent out my original apartment in SP, which was ridiculously oversized. My plan was to move instead to another, smaller apartment that I had recently bought in the neighborhood of Pinheiros. That new apartment is located two minutes by foot from my office and bar. A lot of my life could take place within a half-kilometer radius, eliminating the need for a car even further. In a city with traffic such as SP's, this is worth a lot and a source of regular envy among others, not a few of which spend a couple of hours each day in traffic jams. I have already started to explain why I liked Pinheiros as an investment area. By now, there were more signs of positive change. On the block of my office, two new restaurants opened. Another commercial house that had been for rent for ages, finally rented out and now houses a high-end home appliance store. A couple of other owners put up their houses for sale at prices on average some 50 percent above what I had paid for my office per square meter, and eventually did manage to sell.

In an unintended consequence, my plan to switch apartments led to the end of my relationship with Nandi. She did not appreciate the fact that I considered going through all the trouble of renting out my apartment just to move in by myself again, rather than with her. To be fair, Nandi was very relaxed for a Brazilian girl. Nevertheless, I was acutely aware that we had been dating for a year and a quarter and I knew I would be facing that question most dreaded by all men: "Where is this relationship going?"—no cultural differences here. I was not ready for further commitment, so we took the consequence and broke up, on good terms, and remained friends.

There was considerable interest in my apartment, especially by foreigners looking to come to Brazil. This was a continuing trend. Like in 2009, in 2010 I was contacted by several people from around the world contemplating a move to Brazil. For some reason, that year, that group of people included a disproportionate number of German Internet entrepreneurs. As a side note, with regard to foreigners, there was one other change I noticed: there were now several examples of foreigners whose limited-time expat assignments were up, who previously would have left to go back to their home offices, but who now opted to stay in Brazil, even if it meant having to change their jobs. In any event, foreigners were a good target group for my apartment. They appreciated the central location, and they did not care about the lack of parking spots. The list of potential tenants visiting the apartment included a cofounder of one of the best-known Internet companies in the world (wanting to set up a venture capital office in SP), the chairman and CEO of a Portuguese conglomerate (wanting to expand his Brazilian operations), and the last prince of a European royal dynasty. I was usually out working when they visited. My doorman told me later that one of the potential tenants from abroad had shown up with five bodyguards—clearly there were still stereotypes about the security situation in Brazil among foreigners. The rent that was offered to me implied that the apartment's value had slightly more than doubled over the previous eighteen months, which actually seemed just about fair.

In June the renovation of the bar finally concluded and it looked fantastic—a cozy, classy space just as we had imagined it, featuring custom-made heavy leather sofas, antique wood, crystal chandeliers, and velvet curtains. We had also managed to buy some great leather armchairs in the liquidation auction of a former luxury hotel in SP. The football World Cup was upon us, so we decided to have a soft opening of the bar (without full menu, without publicity, and without full staff) to show some of the matches.

It is difficult to grasp the importance and impact of the football World Cup in Brazil; you need to be there to experience it. During Brazil matches, virtually everything closes, traffic all but dies down, and stock exchange volumes drop off a cliff. It goes without saying that employers, including me, have to give their employees time off to watch the games. If time zones mean that some games are played in the middle of the working day—as was the case this time—you better provide a TV viewing area in your office in order not to risk your employees simply going home. It is also clearly permissible to allow the wearing of national team colors as the business dress code during those days, and possibly face painting too. Customers will not mind anyway—they will probably show up in the same outfit. In this World Cup, after Brazil went out against Holland in the quarterfinals, things quickly went back to normal, except that there was one more big game to watch, fortunately on a Saturday: the quarterfinal between Germany and Argentina. By chance I actually ended up watching that game in Buenos Aires, in an alleged German restaurant (packed with fanatic Argentines), fearing for my life. I was constantly exchanging messages with my friends in SP though. When Germany won 4–0, in the words of one friend, the street scene in SP seemed like Brazil had just won the World Cup. For Brazilians, few things are sweeter than Argentina getting humiliated.

Outside of the World Cup, I have so far not gotten into football in Brazil (i.e., into Brazilian club football). For now, anyway, many of the best Brazilians still play in the foreign leagues, and as a result the quality of league football is typically not yet on par with the quality, say, of the English Premier League or Spain's La Liga. I would expect all of this to change over the next few years, as more local money in Brazil will likely flow into local football, enabling the clubs to hold the good players in the country. In any event, the Brazilian club fans do not care; they are fanatic about their teams. SP and Rio each have various first-league teams, and rivalries are expectedly huge, making local derbies the biggest matches around. One time I watched yet another rather lame 1–1 draw between key SP teams São Paulo FC and Corinthians from the comfort of the HSBC box in the huge Morumbi stadium in SP. An hour after the match was over, we still were not allowed to leave. We were eventually informed that the notorious Corinthians fans were apparently in the process of destroying part of the stadium. Then again, this was all merely par for the course for football-fanatic Latin America. Around the same time, I heard that fans in Buenos Aires had hijacked a public bus to get to their team's match in the stadium quicker.

At the end of July, we officially inaugurated the bar, with an invitation-only event. A live jazz band played, and a DJ kept the crowd going until early in the morning. Immediately after the bar's inauguration, we started opening regularly on Thursday, Friday, and Saturday nights, always offering live music and/or a DJ. We had to find our rhythm and see what happened.

By that time of the year, FinanciarCasa's project pipeline with real estate developers had grown to more than a dozen developments, and we had some fifteen staff. I knew we needed to do a number of things to keep our infrastructure adequate for our new size. We urgently had to hire a dedicated HR person, as I certainly could not deal directly with the issues of that many employees. Brazilian labor laws are very intricate and with any error you make, you risk a potential labor lawsuit, and, as I mentioned, labor courts typically rule in favor of the employee.

FinanciarCasa's business model was in theory self-sustaining in cash terms, but in the vast majority of mortgage processes, we are only paid at the conclusion of the process, sometimes only after several months of work. In the context of the aforementioned growth investment requirements, that created a working capital issue, because we needed to hire the additional staff for new projects obviously at the beginning of the project (not to mention, buy their furniture, computer, etc.). I was also keen to have additional funds to simply accelerate our expansion, of course always at a responsible speed. So I knew it was time to raise funds again, and I started talking to a few parties. Once more, there were serendipities and unexpected referrals. Through a referral from a contact from my hedge fund days, I got to know a former London hedge fund manager who was heavily betting on Brazil and investing in a number of businesses, including launching a mortgage lending operation. He bought an apartment and started spending a considerable amount of his time in SP. He was yet another one of the new breed of entrepreneur expats in Brazil.

I pulled together due diligence materials to get started on the fund-raising process with the new investor.

By that time, I was in need of a vacation. My new girlfriend and I spent a week in Morocco and also made stops in Holland for a wedding, and one day each in London, Paris, and Madrid. If you live more than twelve hours away by plane, you have to be efficient and take advantage of your visits to Europe! Alas, my new relationship did not work out. Fortunately, entrepreneurship really hones your skill to make quick decisions once you have realized what the facts seem to spell out. "Often wrong, but always with 100 percent certainty," as a friend of mine once said. Once we got back from vacation, I broke up with the new girlfriend and I was back to single dating life. I was temporarily exasperated with Brazilian women. I laconically remarked to various friends that I needed to get some relief and date some calmer nationality.

I was not the only one having relationship issues. At regular boys' nights, sometimes only expats and sometimes mixed, there was a lot of comparing of notes regarding relationships. The experiences ranged from harmless, to scary, to outright bizarre. In the more harmless category, one of my friends had been to a family lunch where his girlfriend's mother put he and his girlfriend on the spot, assigning a deadline for her daughter to become pregnant. In the scary category, a friend of a friend had fallen victim to the feared *golpe de barriga* (which roughly translates into "belly scam"), whereby a woman chooses to become pregnant without her partner's consent, often by faking to be on the pill. Finally, in the bizarre category, one of my expat acquaintances found out that his girlfriend's real job was being a high-end escort. None of this dented our love for Brazilian women though. I think we just wrote it off as being acceptable perils of dating, especially in a big-city environment like São Paulo.

While I was on holiday, I noticed something that I had already perceived in 2008 and 2009: vacation away from

Brazil seemed cheaper and cheaper, as the Brazilian real kept appreciating and as the cost of living in SP kept rising. Fortunately, at least that year, there was no new nightclub in SP raising the price bar even further—we at the bar also stuck to a normal, decent price level. As always, additional symbols of new wealth kept springing up. More malls prepared to open. On the automotive front, Aston Martin and Bentley opened dealerships in the city. I heard that Bugatti would start selling its cars in Brazil, too, at a price tag of R$6 million (about US$3.5 million). My cheap auto-buying scheme idea of the year was buying a taxi license. Licensed taxis actually get considerable tax discounts on new cars, translating into something like a 30 percent discount on the normal purchase price of the car. If I got a driver, I would also always be allowed to use the bus lanes, bypassing traffic on main roads. Besides, when not using the car myself, I could send the driver out there "working," earning at least a return on the investment in the car and the taxi license. Because I would likely buy a nice car, say a nice SUV, "my" taxi surely would not have any problem attracting customers. I actually like that idea a lot, but I have not gone through with it so far.

Speaking about the cost of imports in Brazil, and already having spoken about the danger of trying to do too many projects, I came up with one more random idea that year. Given the high import prices for anything ranging from French champagne to iPads in Brazil, it is of course entirely common to ask friends who are traveling to bring along such items from abroad. At some point, I commented to my partner Fernanda that, in order to save on costs at the bar, we should buy our most expensive champagnes and whiskies, of which we only need a few bottles in stock, in this way—by always bringing a few bottles along when we travel abroad, or asking friends who traveled. I figured there should be an institutionalized way to do this, but I could not find an existing one on the Internet. So I came up with the idea for the site bringmethings.com, which is basically a marketplace where people who need something in some place can connect with people who travel to that place and can bring the needed item along. I specified the web platform over a weekend and had it programmed by FinanciarCasa's IT providers, obviously paying out of my personal pocket. Then it became clear to me that this was just the first step, that there needed to be a real business plan, especially a marketing plan, and somebody to execute it, who could not be me. I hate to say it, but bringmethings.com for the moment continues as an orphaned project. I hope to soon find somebody to take care of it, as I do believe it has potential.

At FinanciarCasa, growth continued, most notably in terms of staff size; by the end of 2010, we had about thirty employees. We also started hiring a few interns to help out with various tasks. Interns are a great feature of the otherwise very employer-unfriendly Brazilian labor regulations. Depending on the prestige of the intern's school, and the geographical location, one can typically employ an intern for something like R$800 to R$2,000 (roughly US$450 to US$1,200) per month, but the employer does not have to pay all of the non-salary costs that typically can add up to almost 100 percent of the original salary. The only extra cost is a relatively cheap insurance policy for the intern. The drawbacks are that the intern can technically only work up to six hours per day, and that, since 2008, new regulations limit the number of interns to 20 percent of the number of regular employees.

With the increased number of staff, unfortunately labor problems were also rising. There was a rather undesired increasing level of "flexibility" among the employees with regard to basic rules such as showing up on time in the morning, limiting their lunches to the allotted time, bringing doctors' notes after sick days, etc. Some people, who for various reasons no longer wanted to work at the company, started slacking off and/or having a lot of sick days, trying hard to get fired (which has advantages for them over resigning). A couple of employees simply failed to show up for work one day and never came back, leaving all their work unfinished, and not even offering any assistance in the transfer of their work to other people—in fact, they no longer answered their phones. One of them eventually called in several weeks later, calmly asking about outstanding variable compensation that he thought that he was still due. Even in these cases, Brazilian labor law makes it difficult to fire the employees: while there is an option for terminating employees for "abandoning employment," the employer has to wait for almost one month, while trying to contact the employee via two telegrams and finally an ad in a national newspaper. In general firing employees for cause in Brazil is very difficult, even in circumstances that would clearly seem to warrant it (e.g., when an employee has been found stealing from the company). At the time, we also got our first labor lawsuit; an IT service provider who we had hired for one month for a specific project had done such an unsatisfactory job that we fired him after only two weeks. He sued us in labor court trying to get the full monthly pay—without having a contractual basis, and leaving aside the fact that the labor court was not even the correct venue for his lawsuit. Nevertheless, on the advice of our lawyer, we settled out of court for a small amount. Labor issues in Brazil are complicated and I believe truly hold up entrepreneurship in the country. It pains me to say it, but if I start another company in Brazil, I will try to make it as labor unintensive as possible.

In any event, FinanciarCasa already had a bunch of employees, and, to be fair, many very good and dedicated ones. We owed them structured training and more information on what was going on in the company. Brazilian employees typically need more feedback and more targets than many of their international counterparts. Together with the new HR person, and with the help of other team members, we implemented new initiatives such as a monthly employee newsletter, a monthly staff meeting, an award for employee of the month, biannual 360-degree reviews, and variable performance-based compensation for everybody. The latter is very important to me, and I want to be surrounded by employees who care about it too. That is a recruiting challenge we do not always get right. In all places, but I think especially in Brazil, with its well-known oversized public servant apparatus, there are people with the mentality that it is better to work eight hours straight for a fixed salary than work a little harder and earn a performance-based income. The former group of people often has the illusion of having a right to raises or promotions based solely on how long they have been with the company rather than based on merit (again similar to public servants). At FinanciarCasa we are careful to steer clear of the wannabe public servants.

I also decided to open up a Rio office, based on the demand for our services that I perceived in that market—and not based solely on my desire to spend more time living in Rio, as some of my friends suspected. Rio has a large number of developments, not in the traditional beach areas of Copacabana and Ipanema, where it is virtually impossible to construct new buildings, but in the vast Barra da Tijuca, a beach area about fifteen minutes (without traffic, or sometimes one hour with traffic) south of the traditional beaches. In Barra, space for new buildings is readily available, but it is also further detached and its entertainment options are considerably less charming than those in the traditional areas. Barra is to Copacabana and Ipanema something like Sunny Isles is to South Beach in Miami terms. We first tried to rent office space in Rio's historical center, the Centro. As opposed to SP's Centro, Rio's Centro has held on to its position as the city's main business areas, even though some well-to-do companies have moved to the limited office spaces in Leblon, and some companies have moved to Barra de Tijuca. The rental market in the Centro is very quick, though, due to high demand, and we lost out to other bidders a couple of times. In parallel, I noticed that purchase prices for office space in the Centro were actually quite reasonable, at around R$2,000 to R$4,000 per square meter, depending on exact location and building. To top it off, I had heard repeated anecdotes of companies located in Barra wanting to move back to the Centro because they could not cope with the worsening traffic anymore. Those were enough good data points for me, and I decided to buy rather than rent office space (to be more accurate, I decided to buy office space as a private person and then rent it out to the company). One day, I grabbed my first employee in Rio and we went to talk to all the doormen in all of the office buildings that I liked in the Centro. Sure enough, we found an unadvertised office space for sale, with a postcard view overlooking Rio's iconic Sugarloaf Mountain and the Corcovado Mountain with the Christ the Redeemer statue.

In the meantime, the revised FinanciarCasa website had gone live and was getting something like four thousand visits and around seventy customer e-mail contacts per week. About half of the customer contacts now ask about home equity loans, a brand-new product in Brazil, so far offered by few financial institutions, and virtually unknown by the Brazilian consumers. The growth potential for home equity loans in Brazil is absurd. Penetration is virtually zero, yet on the other hand, if consumers knew about it, there would be a wall of demand. This is because home ownership in Brazil is actually reasonably high; there are many people who own fully paid-off properties and hence have a fair amount of wealth, albeit historically it has been illiquid wealth. On the other side, the well-known loan products available to those who need money often charge exorbitant interest rates, ranging from something like 2.5 percent per month for a personal loan to over 8 percent per month for overdraft credit facilities. For those in need of money, who own a property, home equity is clearly a very attractive option. The problem, as I mentioned, is that most of those potential customers do not even know that the product exists; once more, it is a marketing challenge. Especially, for lower-income classes, the quantitative benefits of home equity over other forms of credit need to be explained explicitly, as many people have developed the bad habit of not even looking at the interest rate of a loan but simply at the absolute amount of the monthly payment; if they can afford that absolute amount, that for many people is all they need to know, never mind the interest rate. Many Brazilian financial institutions and retailers have made a lot of money exploiting this lack of "financial literacy," by offering loans and products at what would elsewhere be considered abusive interest rates. I should note that Brazilian banks lend out using much more responsible criteria than U.S. and European counterparts did before the financial crisis. For example, for a home equity loan, the maximum loan amount is 50 percent of the assessed value of the property, and the borrower always has to document the sources of his or her income.

The bar, JA367, was meanwhile picking up speed, albeit still losing money. We learned very quickly that the key to making money is hosting events, when we can charge high fixed prices. We even hosted one of the get-togethers of InterNations, the expat network, when two hundred people packed the bar beyond its capacity. At least by now, the bar had found some sort of rhythm, we had a decent skeleton staff, and we had some very good music acts, most of them referrals from friends. JA367 had also already been reviewed in most key local newspapers and magazines, and even in the Brazilian edition of *Playboy*. It became my favorite hangout, which makes sense, as it had been designed according to my ideas of what a bar should be like. Yet there were still problems. Most gravely, we still needed to find an industry-experienced general manager to free my partner, Fernanda, and me from spending too much management time on the bar. Our few residential neighbors, albeit clearly living in mixed commercial zoning, bent over backward to try to shut us down. Virtually every day that we opened, they sent the police around for some reason. Sometimes it was just for noise, which we easily solved by closing some doors and turning down the music a little. Sometimes, the neighbors got more creative in their denunciations, including when they claimed that we ran a brothel (admittedly, our prevalence of red lighting may have contributed to this; on a another night, a couple showed up asking the doorman whether we were a swingers' club). One evening, before opening, a couple of policemen in body armor and with machine guns showed up as they had been told that we ran a bingo outfit (bingo, as I mentioned, was at that point illegal and run by organized crime, and no longer by nice people like my Swiss friend). In October, we almost got closed down because our despachante had not gotten all the necessary permits after all. He had in fact provided a rather lousy incomplete service and graciously offered to fix all the errors—for an extra fee. He was one of the few professionals in Brazil that I had hired who did not come to me via a chain-of-trust referral, which was clearly a mistake. We swiftly switched to a despachante whose name we got via referral, and our permit issue got sorted out within a week.

The JA367 Lounge Bar – my pet project in São Paulo

With everything that was going on at FinanciarCasa and at the bar, I was actually glad not to have a girlfriend, as I would not have been able to give her the proper time and attention. I was back to dating, juggling various women, always trying to ensure that not more than one of them would show up at my bar on a given night, which actually turned out to be quite a difficult logistical challenge and went wrong more than once. I wondered how other people handled this problem. I asked one of my Brazilian guy friends, how another mutual expat friend of ours, arguably the uncrowned king of multiple simultaneous dating in SP, managed to stay clear of this type of situation. My friend shot back, "Oh, him, but he's regionally diversifying." I did not have to ask any further, I knew various expat friends who employed the same strategy. Like I said before, Brazil is a village and everybody knows everybody else—within *certain clusters* at least. In other words, if you date a girl from the central Jardins area in SP, but your other dates are from a variety of suburbs more on the outskirts of SP, you can be reasonably comfortable that there are no overlaps in the girls' circles of friends. You also do not have to run any risks of showing up in a popular restaurant or bar and running into another girl, because you do not have to take the suburb girls to the same places. I frankly preferred continuing to run the risk of having two girls from the same circle of friends run into each other and just be honest about what I was doing.

One of the girls I was dating finally offered up a theory on what had previously baffled me—why it was always the women who get blamed whenever there is cheating. "It's in men's nature to cheat—they cannot do otherwise," she started to elaborate. I just understood Brazilian jealousy a tiny bit more but replied, "Ummm, I'm not sure I necessarily agree—" She cut me off and continued undeterred, "Hence, any woman who gives them the opportunity to cheat is the guilty party." I was about as baffled as I was when my friend had explained the rationale for going to brothels to me, but who was I to disagree.

That fall, Brazil elected a new president, Dilma Rousseff, the daughter of a Bulgarian immigrant, former cabinet chief, and President Lula's anointed successor. She was also a former Marxist guerilla fighting the military dictatorship, a period during which she robbed banks, among other illicit activities. Some of my local friends commented how they thought a "former terrorist" was not fit to be the country's president. I think partly because I am German, that kind of comment annoyed me, as, after all, Dilma was fighting an illegitimate dictatorship that suppressed freedoms, and did many worse things. I also feel that at least sometimes this is part of an unfortunate Brazilian tendency to blame the current government, and politicians in general, for anything that is wrong in the country. On the other hand, many Brazilians I know make little effort to get involved in the political process themselves in order to help change these perceived shortcomings. For example, the run-off election for president fell on a long holiday weekend, and probably the majority of people I know opted for beach over voting (despite technically mandatory voting). As a side note, that fact in itself may have cost opposition candidate José Serra any chance of winning, as his voters were more numerous among the affluent classes (who do things such as weekend trips to the beaches), while Dilma's are more numerous among the poorer parts of society. People in general are just not that politicized, which is a real shame, as there are so many qualified, energetic, and entrepreneurial individuals who could really make a difference to their country.

To be fair, there are admirable exceptions. A couple of friends of mine, among other people, founded a new political party in late 2010, whose philosophy it is to vote normal citizens, not career politicians, into office, and to increase efficiency in government. I feel like this might be just one of the first of what I hope will be many new political initiatives in Brazil, most of which, I think, will be driven by a newly emancipated middle class eager to exercise political power to ensure that the conditions that created its newfound wealth will continue in the future. I should also mention the Brazilian press, which does an excellent job of monitoring the government, much better than their peers in many other countries that I have seen. I, on the other hand, consider myself a very politicized person. Besides the presidency, there were a lot of other public offices up for election that October, including governorships and parliament positions. I hated the fact that I could not vote. I invested in the country, I paid taxes, I felt I should be able to vote too. I started researching how I could fast-track a naturalization process in order to become a Brazilian citizen.

I finished the year with FinanciarCasa in growth but also with feeling responsible for its increasing number of employees. I also had a promising new bar that needed at least some attention. I was in the process of renovating three apartments and one office. It all seemed a far cry from that time when I arrived in Brazil with no responsibilities, most of my net worth in liquid investments and a stable relationship. My love life remained complicated; I had no idea where it would lead. I was starting to consider using the guidance of astrologists and/or clairvoyants, which is a very Brazilian thing to do.

These were objectively stressful times, even if I consciously chose and liked the stress. That year I could not do without going for a detox on the island in Thailand. On the one-hour ride to São Paulo's international airport, I got one of those taxi drivers who make for good conversation. He was a part-time independent taxi driver and part-time police officer, saving up money to buy a country house, and studying as well to work in a higher-paid branch of the police. Without my prompting, he entered into the topic of corruption and explained how he refused to receive bribes. He told me a story about how he had recently driven a federal politician on a long limousine ride, costing some R$150. Naturally, the driver wrote out a receipt of the R$150 expense for the politician. However, the politician asked him to give him three more identical receipts.

My driver told me he just replied, "So I guess effectively you want this ride for free?"

"What do you mean?" the politician replied confused.

"You know, I'm a taxpayer too," my driver responded, after which the politician exited the car, irritated and without the extra receipts. It is people like my taxi driver, a member of the new middle class, who make me optimistic about the future of politics in Brazil after all.

CHAPTER 9

THE BRAZILIAN DREAM TAKES OFF

I will remember 2011 as the year when the flow of foreign immigrants to Brazil really picked up.

In a no longer surprising episode, a couple of English girls started talking to me recently on the Heathrow Express in London, where I had just arrived from Rio:

"You're so tanned! Where are you from?" one of them asked.

"I live in Brazil." The answer is almost automatic by now.

"Oh really?! I want to move there too!"

"Why's that?"

"Well, this place isn't happening right now."

Lots of people outside of Brazil must be thinking about moving to Brazil; that is clear also from other anecdotes. A Spanish friend told me that Portuguese courses in Madrid and Barcelona are booked out, and that the Brazilian embassy in Spain got so many information requests about coming to Brazil that it posted a clarifying statement explaining that there is a bureaucratic visa process involved and that speaking some Portuguese is not enough. I myself get at least one e-mail a week from somebody curious about moving to Brazil; that is significantly up from a couple of years ago, when there were sporadic e-mails once every few months.

More important, besides just thinking about it, more and more people *are* actually moving to Brazil. The official data shows that—visa applications have skyrocketed recently, and it is also visible to me in my life in SP as most of the new arrivals are entrepreneurs who sooner or later cross my path. Most of them look to set up Internet ventures. There is a German who started an online designer furniture store (oppa.com.br), a German and Portuguese duo currently setting up a price comparison website for financial services (taclaro.com.br), two recent American MBA graduates who founded an online baby goods site (baby.com.br), and many others. In fact, there were so many examples, that local business magazine *ISTOÉ Dinheiro* ran a cover article in 2011 featuring some of their stories, called (translated) "The garage is here." For those with entrepreneurial ambitions but who want to have a strong supportive structure and financing (traded off against a smaller equity stake), Internet incubators such as Germany's Rocket Internet have already helped to start various businesses in Brazil (e.g., the local Groupon clone and an online shoe store) and are continuing to recruit "founders." Virtually everybody comes to Brazil making use of the aforementioned investor visa option. It feels like a gold rush mentality, with people streaming toward the perceived opportunity. By now, when I speak to the most recent arrivals and tell them how I arrived in late 2007, I get comments like, "Wow, you were on the first plane down."

New events catering to this crowd have sprung up, such as the monthly BR New Tech get-togethers that focus on technology start-ups—here, the contingent of foreigners is strong and noticeable. Besides potential entrepreneurs, foreign venture capital firms are arriving in the country in increasing numbers. While actual local offices of such VCs are still scarce, their partners seem to come down to Brazil very regularly now. I myself met with four different U.S.-based VC funds in 2011. By now, the first investments of such VCs in local Brazilian companies have been made, and the permanent offices are just a matter of time.

I find all of this vibrant activity hugely exciting and inspirational. In fact, it strengthens my urge to try yet another venture. As a consequence, I have to control myself in order not to fall into that trap of ending up overextending myself and taking on more projects than I can handle with quality and responsibility. For me, the first priority is still to bring FinanciarCasa, the mortgage company, to a successful conclusion (such as a sale or at least a stable, cash-generative growth pattern), which in turn will make it easier for me to find partners and investors for the next potential venture. Even though growth has been slower and more challenging than I would have hoped, I still very much believe this is possible. If I did not, I would be ruthless in shutting the company down and starting a new project; a market full of opportunities such as Brazil is unlikely to come around many times during my lifetime, and I cannot waste time on the wrong project.

FinanciarCasa completed its second funding round during the second quarter of 2011, continued to grow, and turned itself into a higher quality business, I think. In the process, we took some decisive actions, including changing almost half of our staff (we ended up with fewer employees and significantly higher productivity), getting rid of some real estate developer clients that we judged to be not profitable enough, and simplifying our consumer-facing website. Most important, we are looking for a real game changer to accelerate the company's growth—in our case, this will be a merger that will take the company significantly more online.

Yet even though my current attention is fully focused on bringing FinanciarCasa to a successful conclusion (I am now even considering selling my participation in the bar JA367 to eliminate this minor distraction), I cannot help to think about potential future entrepreneurial projects. I have quite a few ideas, but I will not talk about them here, as they are still at the relatively early stage and require more thinking. What I can and will talk about, though, and what is an important part of thinking about future entrepreneurial projects, is some of the things I have learned so far from my first entrepreneurial experience in Brazil. Here are a few, in no particular order:

THINK BIG, AS BIG AS BRAZIL

Brazil is a huge country, with a huge market. There are billion-dollar businesses out there still to be built. Think about it: Brazil almost has two hundred million people. Is it so unreasonable to think of a business that, for example, reaches 5 percent of the population, and those 5 percent spend R$10 a month on your product or service? In that case, you have a business with more than R$1bn of sales. There is no reason to limit yourself to something small. Get your return-on-time right: do not spend your precious time on something that is unnecessarily small. It is easy to fall into this trap because there are simply so many opportunities around, on all size levels. I already mentioned some potential businesses that came across my radar screen and that I discarded because the economics did not seem meaningful enough in the return-on-time framework (e.g., the real estate broker in Rio, or the real estate fund for high-net-worth individuals). There are other examples. For example, at some point I noticed that there are no gourmet cookies in Brazil. I am pretty sure gourmet cookies would work here, and I ran through some basic calculations about a franchised gourmet cookie chain, but I could not get to meaningful enough size numbers. That does not mean that any of these businesses are bad businesses.

Neither does it mean that any of them could not provide you with a good, or potentially very good, livelihood. I am saying that you should choose your project carefully and always ask yourself if there is not something better out there (of course keeping other criteria in mind, including applicability of previous experiences and contacts that you have, government regulations, etc.). Shoot for the stars.

GET SUFFICIENT CAPITAL

If you think big enough, you will likely need a reasonable amount of capital. Many businesses will need at least R$5 million to R$10 million to get started credibly. Take advantage of the current positive market environment and strong interest in Brazil and try to raise this capital. Keep in mind that market environment can always change, sometimes quickly. Besides, repeated fund-raising can be a huge distraction from operations. There are other reasons I could cite, but you get the point.

PAY UP FOR GOOD STAFF AND ADVISORS

Like in probably any place, there is a huge quality variance in terms of available staff. Do not skimp on good staff. If you pay peanuts, you get monkeys. Take advantage of the fact that there is such strong interest in Brazil on the part of people at the moment too. There is a whole class of people with excellent qualifications who want to be entrepreneurs here, but for whatever reason they may fail to become entrepreneurs. Maybe because they will fail to secure the necessary backing. Or maybe because they do not have the guts to go through with it by themselves. Whatever the reason, that class of people should be a good recruiting pool, as these people will probably appreciate the chance to get exposure to the entrepreneurial option via working for your start-up (for a little bit of equity, and a reasonable salary). Pay up for good advisors too; I already mentioned that in Brazil it is often easier to just go for the highest quality and most expensive option.

GET CREDIBLE BRAZILIAN PARTNERS
This is especially true if you are a recent arrival. Like I mentioned, there are benefits to having the nonlocal view, but there is undisputed value in having people on board who grew up in the culture. Remember the "Brazil is a village" aspect and the useful relationships that a local partner should bring along if you choose the right one. For fund-raising, too, potential investors will probably penalize you if you are *just* a bunch of recently arrived gringos who hardly speak any Portuguese. And, no, having been in Brazil for Carnival and having done a project on Brazil during your MBA are not enough.

TRY TO HAVE LOW LABOR INTENSITY
I already explained why. Again, it pains me to say it, as I genuinely like the aspect of creating jobs. I hold out the hope that, one day, labor laws in Brazil will be more conducive to starting up businesses.

These are just some examples of good lessons. If you have any specific queries, feel free to post them on the book's Facebook page. If I judge your query to be of general interest, I will include the query and answer in future editions of this book.

Looking back more generally over my four years here, I believe Brazil has delivered on virtually all of the original professional and lifestyle criteria. There are tons of business opportunities around. These opportunities *are* accessible to foreigners, as not only my own case but also those of now various other foreigners prove. Beyond merely my start-up mortgage company, my real estate investments here have worked out very well. I love my lifestyle in Brazil—in no particular order, the food, the outdoor sports options, the beaches, the domestic help, the vibrant arts scene in SP. I am also in a new relationship with a Brazilian girl and very happy in that realm of life too.

In the jargon of my old profession as a trader: my Brazil trade "has worked." But will it continue to work? Or is the trade already over? Is it "time to sell?"

Here, I have to strike one slightly more cautious note about all the increase in entrepreneurial activity, principally by foreigners, in 2011. I am by nature a contrarian and, purely from that perspective, felt more comfortable when Brazil was "less discovered." Nowadays, Brazil is not a contrarian's story. If you want something like Brazil in its earlier stage in 2007, today perhaps you should move to Angola or a similar country. The BR New Tech meetings, where everybody seems to have some idea and everybody seems to be on the cusp of starting a business, remind me eerily of the "First Tuesday" Internet get-togethers that existed at the very end of the last Internet bubble. R$10 million venture capital valuations on mere business plans (no product, no clients, no revenue) are very nice for entrepreneurs, but I am also not sure how normal or sustainable they are. In real estate, some areas probably have seen price increases that were too sharp and have to at least consolidate at those new price levels.

Then again, whenever I look back at fundamentals, such as market penetration data for many products and services, I feel relatively assured that Brazil is only at the beginning and has a long way to go. By and large, the macroeconomic data is still solid, albeit there recently has been a slowdown in growth and the single biggest threat, in my mind, is the relatively low productivity, which brings us back to things like labor laws. There will probably be some challenges and even excesses on the way, and the occasional bust and shakeout, but I guess that is normal—you just have to try to personally steer clear of those. In order to soothe my contrarian conscience, I sold some of my real estate in 2011, and I also changed a reasonable amount of money out of reais, first into gold, later on in the year into U.S. dollars. Beyond these mere investment position adjustments, I never had any doubts about Brazil; there was never any thought about moving away. I still believe in the trade.

Besides, even the lifestyle aspects of Brazil are further improving. For example, Rio de Janeiro now seems to have seriously started to tackle its crime problem, by systematically clearing its favelas of criminals, installing permanent police stations, and investing in basic community infrastructure inside the favelas, ranging from street signs to cinemas and football fields. In contrast to the past, favela inhabitants now appear to welcome the police, and to actually help them (e.g., by denouncing the criminals).

Then, of course, there is the other side of the equation—the world outside of Brazil. Europe clearly has issues that have not been worked out yet and may still take years to work through. The only major European country that I believe will come out fine in any event, due to its stable macroeconomic position and its wealth of high-quality businesses, is Germany. The U.S. economy I think will do fine due to its unrivaled innovative power and its high productivity. However, in the United States there is an ongoing disturbing trend, also increasingly present in Europe, of growing societal inequality (with regard to income and wealth) and of decimating a once large and vibrant middle class. As a vivid illustration: over the recent years, looking at the Gini index of wealth distribution of a country, the United States has become an ever more unequal society while equality in Brazil has ever increased, due to the social measures of the last few Brazilian governments; if trends continue, in the not-too-distant future the United States could be a more unequal society than Brazil.

Probably nobody would have predicted this a few years ago. I find these trends highly disturbing and just plain sad. In my old sector, finance, hundreds of thousands of jobs have been lost, and the suspicion is that a good part of those losses are actually structural (i.e., those jobs will not come back). Then there are a few potential black-swan-type events in the world that are just completely unpredictable but could have a significant impact (e.g., a potential Israeli attack on Iran's nuclear facilities or military action in the Koreas). In summary, there is so much uncertainty that I have less of a view on the future than at any other point in time since I actively started thinking about this type of stuff. I hardly even know what type of currency to hold my cash in anymore (but usually opt for a mix of Brazilian real and U.S. dollars). However, one of the few strong beliefs I do have is that Brazil is a good place and haven to be in at this point, and that I do love my life here in any event. So I am staying.

An increasing number of people are having similar thoughts, and that probably means that the immigrant inflow will continue. More and more people will arrive here in search of the Brazilian Dream. Like in the United States about a hundred years ago, I believe this is a good thing for the country.

Epilogue Part 1: Concepts Of Home

São Paulo is the eighth place in my life where I am keeping a home, the former seven being Freiburg, Dusseldorf, Philadelphia, New York, London, Sydney, and Tokyo. I am saying "keeping a home" instead of something like "that is my home" because the latter does not *feel* right. Which brings me to an interesting point and one that is worth reflecting upon for anybody contemplating a big move: what does it take to call a place your *home*?

If we think about intuitive and common answers to this question, they would probably include: where you were born, where you grew up, where you went to school, where you studied, where you married and started your own family, where you work, where the majority of your friends live, and the like. Now, once upon a time, and still today for a vast majority of people, it so happens that most and perhaps all of the statements above reference one and the same place. For many of my friends in São Paulo, for example, this still holds true: they were born, brought up, and educated here; typically live with their family until they marry; and then start their own family home here. Naturally the majority of their friends live here. All of these elements bind you to one place, where you are inherently rooted.

I personally have many times been accused of having no roots. I grew up in Germany, where my family still lives, I went to school in the United States, I worked all around the world, nowadays my friends are scattered around the world, and so on.

I will defiantly say—I feel none the poorer. Take the example of friends. Sure, I have left behind "friends" in every place that I moved away from, but I believe that the real ones will care enough to stay in touch with you, and the fleeting ones will naturally fall away, which, if anything, I regard as useful filtering.

But this is just one example. I think in every way, the act of removing yourself from your traditional comfort zone will force you to think about yourself and the world and the people that surround you, and you will hopefully gain a lot of insights. And it might be that, just like in Brazilian author Paulo Coelho's *Alchemist*, you may travel far away only to realize that your original home is where you are supposed to be. That is perfectly fine too.

In the end, I found my new definition of home: it is where you can realize your dreams, whatever they may be.

Epilogue Part 2: Explore, Dream, Discover, And Write About It

Sometimes people actually tell me they admire me for having had the guts to just leave and move to Brazil and start a new life here. I feel somewhat flattered, but mostly I think that is a ridiculous statement. What I have done, in one way or another, millions have done before me, just in Brazil over six million since 1872 (when census data began). Looking at investor visas in Brazil, the number already jumped from 197 investor visas granted in 2004 to 1,336 granted in 2007 and has since further increased sharply. And I certainly will not be the last one. Throughout history, there has always been emigration to the lands of opportunity of the time, away from less privileged regions—this time will not be different. I fully expect many more people to come to Brazil in the coming years. And, by the way, it will not only be Brazil; I know Western people who have moved to Singapore or Hong Kong and are raising their kids to speak Mandarin as one of their first languages. I even recently read that there is now a new wave of Irish immigrants arriving in New York.

Many of the historical emigrants left their countries because of economic necessity and some even because of persecution, and not on a whim, with plenty of resources, like I did. Some of their stories have been written down, and are surely worth reading; many have not. But independent of whether an individual story happens to have been documented, I am certain that in some way all of their journeys have been incredible. All the emigrants had to plan, make hard decisions along the way, and ultimately build a new life. For every single one, there must have been moments of exuberance, joy, doubt, boredom, fear, sadness, regret, anticipation, and possibly every other human emotion that exists. When you force yourself out of your comfort zone in such an extreme way, life is lived in a very concentrated form. As a consequence, if you let it happen, your outward journey will also become an inward journey, in that you will get to know yourself better, your role in the universe, your relationships with other people. Therefore, I urge you to enjoy every part of the journey instead of merely focusing on some end result, such as what your life may look like once you have successfully established yourself in your new home. The journey is indeed the destination. Reflect on it often, and maybe at some point even write it down; your children and grandchildren one day will probably love to read it.

In the words of the quote at the beginning of the book, go "explore, dream, discover." It is worth it, you owe it to yourself, and you can do it.

EPILOGUE PART 2: EXPLORE, DREAM, DISCOVER, AND WRITE ABOUT IT

Made in the USA
Charleston, SC
30 August 2013